CW01021951

# BOEING 767

# BOEING 767

## Philip Birtles

**Airlife**
England

First published in the UK in 1999
by Airlife Publishing Ltd

**British Library Cataloguing-in-Publication Data**
A catalogue record for this book
is available from the British Library

ISBN 1 85310 946 0

Printed in Singapore by Kyodo Printing Co (S'pore) Pte Ltd

**Airlife Publishing Ltd**
101 Longden Road, Shrewsbury, SY3 9EB, England
E-mail: airlife@airlifebooks.com
Website: www.airlifebooks.com

COVER: First deliveries outside the USA were to Air Canada in October 1982 who had placed an initial order for ten 767-200s. Air Canada 767-233ER C-GDSP powered by the P&W JT9D-7R4D engines is seen on finals to London Heathrow in April 1992. *Philip Birtles*

PREVIOUS PAGE: Britannia 767-204ER; today this aircraft is Air Seychelles EC-GHM Palma de Mallorca. *Boeing*

BELOW: Qantas 767-338ER VH-OGF. *Qantas*

No work of this nature can be achieved without the help of many people, despite them often having other pressing priorities. I would like to thank Doug Webb and Debbie Heathers-Stiteler in the Everett PR organisation of the Boeing Commercial Airplane Group for their help and hospitality during my visit to Everett. Also Bob and Sandy Hood, good 'Comet' friends who also provided hospitality and organised an unforgettable visit. My old friend Peter 'Cob' Crossley gave enthusiastic support during our stay in the Seattle area, making sure we saw as much of Boeing as possible.

My visit to Hong Kong was a double pleasure, as it not only allowed me to share some time with my wife Martha on one of her extended absences from home, but I was able to picture the operations at Kai Tak before it finally closed. I would also like to thank all the airline Marketeers who so kindly responded to my request for photos, and the photo coverage would not have been complete without the enthusiastic and willing support of Nick Granger. The airside shots of the Leisure International 767-300ER at London Gatwick would not have been achieved without the help of Katherine Carlton-Smyth of Leisure, Kate Rogers of Shandwick and Louise Hume in the Gatwick Press Office. Finally, I would like to thank the series editor, Simon Forty, with whom I have worked for many years, for creating an excellent product, and selecting me to participate in the programme from the start.

**Philip Birtles**
Stevenage, September 1998

# CONTENTS

# INTRODUCTION

For such a traditional looking airliner, the Boeing 767 has been, and continues to be a successful programme, both for the manufacturer and the operators. Progressive developments of the basic airframe, together with engine power and efficiency, has allowed increased payload, greater range and improved economy. One of the early challenges was to achieve long range twin jet operations over oceans, achieving up to 120 minutes diversion time from the nearest suitable airfield.

The original 767-200 is no longer available, but the -200ER, -300 and -300ER are still in production, with the even longer 767-400ER in the advanced design stage. In addition to being an effective passenger carrier, the Boeing 767 has also been adapted to the cargo role, launched in its most basic version by UPS, but available to the full specification as operated by Asiana. Other airframes are also being converted from the passenger to the cargo role.

Like the Boeing 707 before it, the 767 has been adapted to the military role, the first example being the E-767 AWACS for Japan, but equally the 767 is on offer as a tanker/transport for the USAF as the existing KC-135s reach the end of their service lives. By the end of July 1998, 828 Boeing 767s had been ordered, with 709 delivered and future developments should take the 767 programme towards the 1,000 aircraft total.

## BOEING

William Edward Boeing, the son of a German father and a Viennese mother, and born in Detroit on 1 October 1881 studied as an engineer, but settled in Hoquiam, Washington in 1903, to start a successful lumber business. Bill Boeing met Conrad Westervelt, and as their friendship grew, they both became interested in aviation, and on 4 July 1915, they both took their first flight with a barnstorming pilot in a Curtiss seaplane. After a few more flights, Boeing commented that he thought he could build a better aircraft, and that was how it all began.

After the first somewhat rudimentary design, and the departure of Westervelt, Bill Boeing formed the Pacific Aero Products Company on 15 July 1916. As a result of improvements to the original design, the two seat Model C floatplane was produced, and following America's entry into World War I the US Navy ordered 50 as trainers in a contract worth $575,000 starting the company in business, and was then renamed the Boeing Airplane Company. The new name was painted on the red building used as the company headquarters and factory, which is now preserved as the Red Barn at the Seattle Museum of Flight.

With the signing of the Armistice, Boeing, like many other aviation companies suffered a drastic loss of business, and to avoid shutting down altogether started work producing furniture, but did build one aircraft, the B-1 flying boat. This aircraft was flown by Boeing and Eddie Hubbard on the first international air mail flight in North America on 3 March 1919 from Victoria BC to Seattle with 60 letters. This was Boeing's first step into commercial air transport, and the company struggled on to the end of 1921, when a contract was won to build some bombers for the Army followed by a number of other military aircraft.

Boeing's first commercial aircraft was the Model 40A mailplane which was developed at the time the US Government passed the Contract Air Mail Act on 2 February 1925, giving birth to the US airline industry. Not only did Boeing produce a suitable mailplane, but decided to operate it themselves, the Model 40A having two seats for passengers, as well as carrying the mail. They made a successful bid for the Chicago to San Francisco air route, inaugurated by Boeing Air Transport (BAT) on 1 July 1927, who later merged with Pacific Air Transport, adding the Seattle to Los Angeles air route.

Towards the end of 1928 a merger was proposed between Boeing, BAT and Pratt & Whitney, including Chance Vought, and Hamilton and Standard Steel — two propeller manufacturers, all coming under the holding company of United Aircraft & Transport Corporation. Later Stearman, Northrop and Sikorsky were added to this diverse aeronautical organisation. When further airlines were added to the organisation, they were merged under the banner of United Air Lines.

Meanwhile the Boeing Company continued to produce commercial aircraft, their first practical monoplane being the streamlined low wing Monomail designed as a combined mail and cargo aircraft and having a retractable undercarriage. Although the aircraft was not a commercial success, it did lead to the technologically advanced Boeing 247 all metal twin engine airliner. United placed a launch order for 60 247s to compete with the slower TWA's Ford Trimotors and American Airways Condor biplanes. When TWA and American approached Boeing to order 247s, they could not be delivered for over a year, while the United order was being satisfied, resulting in TWA turning to Douglas, who produced the even better DC-2 14 passenger airliner, later leading to the DC-3. With room for only 10 passengers, the 247 could not compete. The disadvantages of tying a manufacturer as sole supplier to an airline began to become apparent.

American Government legislation settled the problem with the Air Mail Act of 1934 which stated that no aircraft or engine

RIGHT: The first Boeing 767 was rolled out from the final assembly hall at Everett on 4 August 1981, by which time orders for the 211 passenger airliner had reached 173 from 17 airlines. *Boeing*

manufacturer should be connected in any way with an airline. Because of suggestions of previous connivance in obtaining mail contracts most of the existing airlines and their senior executives were banned from future operation, which would have reduced the American airline industry to a number of small operators unable to raise the investment to purchase new aircraft. The airline problem was overcome by exploiting a loop hole in the Act, allowing airlines to change their names, the United airline subsidiary becoming United Air Lines Transport.

Although the Boeing Company regained its independence, Bill Boeing had had enough. He had already made it common

knowledge that he wished to retire at 50, and was three years beyond that. Boeing therefore retired in 1934 from the company he founded, severing all connections, including selling his stock, spending his remaining years at leisure, before dying of a heart attack on 28 September 1956 just when the company was to enter the jet age.

Despite the enforced split up of the United Aircraft & Transport Corporation, the different organisations previously within the Group continued to co-operate with each other over the years, United Airlines becoming regular users of Boeing airliners, although not exclusively, as well as often helping to define the overall specification, and placing the launch order.

These airliners were often powered by Pratt & Whitney engines, who themselves became part of the United Technologies Corporation.

During the run up, and for the duration of World War II, the big success for Boeing was the B-17 Flying Fortress. Although this was designed entirely as a war machine, used extensively on the hazardous daylight bombing campaign in Europe, the large numbers produced by American industry, gave Boeing a vast new production capability. From the B-17 followed the longer range B-29 used in the Pacific campaign, and from which was developed Boeings only piston engine post war airliner, the double deck Stratocruiser using the wings, engine and tail of the B-29 Super Fortress wedded to a new fuselage. However the Stratocruiser was only produced in relatively small numbers totalling 55 for commercial use as Douglas had developed their wartime transport aircraft into the DC-4, DC-6 and ultimate DC-7 family and Lockheed had progressively refined the Constellation family. The Stratocruiser did see extensive service as the C-97 military transport and KC-97 flight refuelling tanker, and a small number were modified as outsize cargo aircraft, known as the Guppy and Super Guppy.

Boeing meanwhile had been much more involved with the development of jet bombers for the USAF, starting with the advanced B-47 Stratojet six jet highly swept wing bomber, leading to the much larger eight jet B-52, the later versions of which are still in front line service with the USAF. Over 2,000 B-47s were produced, and 744 B-52s were built, the first making its maiden flight on 15 April 1952, these two aircraft giving Boeing a great deal of large jet designing and development experience.

The world's first commercial jet airliner was the Comet, produced by de Havilland in 1949, followed by service entry with BOAC in 1952, giving Britain a significant lead. However, the structural problems with the early Comets resulted in a radical redesign, and the lessons learned were to benefit the aerospace industry as a whole, including Boeing. While de Havilland were producing the Comet 4, Boeing were already busy with their first jet transport under the company designation Model 367. This started as a development of the C-97 Stratocruiser, but by the time it had become the Model 367-80, the 80th study configuration, it bore no relationship with the earlier design.

Other developments of the B-47 had already been looked at as a possible jet transport, but not progressed with as the Model 367 programme showed better economics. Although the programme adopted the company designation 707, for commercial security reasons the prototype was always referred to as the Model 367-80 in the belief that the competition would assume that the aircraft was an improved C-97.

Boeing initiated work on the private venture -80 prototype on 20 May 1952, just as the Comet 1s were entering service, and rolled out the prototype on 14 May 1954, the maiden flight being two months later on 15 July. Following an evaluation by the USAF the first of a number orders was placed in September 1954 as the KC-135A jet tanker-transports, allowing some sharing of the production tooling as well as a share in development costs, maintaining competitive prices for both military and commercial versions. The launch order for the civil 707 was from PanAm, who put the new airliner into commercial

RIGHT: The Boeing 767 was designed and developed at the same time as the narrow bodied 757 which was produced at the Renton factory to the east of Boeing Field. *Flying Colours* 757-200ER G-FCLE is seen on the flight line at Renton in May 1998. *Philip Birtles*

service on 26 October 1958 across the North Atlantic. The 707 therefore brought the Boeing Company firmly into the jet age with an aircraft that was faster than the pioneering Comet, and available at reasonable prices.

From the 707 was sired the regional trijet 727 with the same cabin section and the twin jet 737 which is the world's best selling airliner and still being developed for future markets. All these airliners were produced at the Renton factory, now termed as the 'Narrow Body' facility, and the 757, with the same fuselage section as the 727 now shares the factory floor with the new generation 737s. With the coming of the Boeing 747 Jumbo Jet, a whole new factory was constructed at Everett, becoming the 'Wide Body' facility to which has been added the 767 and 777 production lines in custom made new buildings. Meanwhile during 1997 Boeing took over their erstwhile competitor, McDonnell Douglas, pulling all the major American airliner manufacture into one organisation, with the competition coming from Airbus in Europe.

# 1 EVOLUTION

The Boeing 767 wide-body airliner involved the company in considerable investment, sharing the development dollars with the narrow-bodied Boeing 757. The two new aircraft were designed at the same time by different teams, with the 757 built in the Renton 'Narrow Body' factory, and the 767 is produced at the vast Everett factory, initially constructed for the Boeing 747. The two aircraft have very little in common, apart from the flightdeck and handling, which allows crews to be qualified on both types, saving training costs for airlines with both types in their fleet.

The evolution of the Boeing 767 took over 10 years in a changing market place, where the services of a reliable crystal ball would have been welcome. During the late 1960s and early 1970s, Boeing, as well as the aerospace and air transport industries as a whole, experienced a traumatic downturn in business due to the oil crisis. The Boeing 747 was just entering service providing an increase in capacity for long range routes which was not completely needed at the time. To save the company, Boeing cut their workforce by two thirds to 36,000 people over a period of three years, but it was during this difficult period that the New Aircraft Program was formed in 1970-71. The task was to attempt to predict market requirements for the next

10 to 15 years, and to conceive a family of new airliners to replace or compliment those in service at the time.

The first mention of the Boeing 767 came in August 1971 with the release of an artists impression of an airliner with an area ruled fuselage, and all flying surfaces with high degrees of sweepback. With capacity for up to 200 passengers, the four-engine aircraft would be capable of cruising at Mach 0.98. The engines were located in two underwing pods and two on the rear fuselage. The Boeing 767 evolved under the designation of the Type 751, and later became a high augmentor type wing layout to achieve STOL performance, and also a T-tail layout with four underwing podded engines. With a predicted in service date of the mid-1970s, cruising speed became Mach 0.8 for ranges between 500 miles and 800 miles (805 and 1,287km). The studies were shared with Aeritalia, with production lines planned in the USA and Italy.

The original STOL concept of operating from 2,500ft (762m) runways was dropped as uneconomic, the alternative Boeing Aeritalia BA-751 being studied as a Quiet Short Haul (QSH) airliner for operation from downtown or secondary airports with 4,000-6,000ft (1,219-1,829m) runways. Reduction in engine noise was a primary requirement, with the added bonus of increased economy and efficiency. However, the concentration on airfield performance was found to be uneconomic, and in September 1972 a new airliner programme was

BELOW: The Boeing 757 has been very popular with the world's airlines with orders for 922 aircraft and 810 delivered by the end of July 1998. Northwest 757-200 N536US is seen at Detroit in May 1998. *Philip Birtles*

announced under the designation of the Boeing 7X7.

The revised object was to determine the specification of the aircraft to meet the airline requirements from the mid-1970s, and in early 1973 Boeing made presentations to a number of airlines in an effort to establish some common parameters by the middle of the year. However, demand for the 727 increased in mid-1973, and there was concern that any decision on a new type might reduce demand for existing airliners, the time scale being changed to an early 1974 launch for service entry at the end of 1977. Even this programme was overly optimistic, as project development continued for another four years before the 7X7 was to emerge as a firm design.

Quietness of operation was an important goal, and as well as being powered by the new high by-pass fan engines with their relatively low exhaust velocity. Other factors, such as the installation on the airframe, acoustic linings and intake and exhaust geometry all played their part. The 7X7 evolved into a medium range twin-jet powered by a pair of 40,000 to 43,000lb (178-191kN) thrust engines in the class of the General Electric CF-6, the Rolls-Royce RB211 and the Pratt & Whitney JT9D. The basic medium-range aircraft was planned to be able to carry 140 passengers over distances of some 2,877 miles (4,630km), but interest began to grow in greater ranges as a result of the analysis of airline response. In this case a three-engine layout was considered with seating for about 200 passengers in six or seven-abreast tourist layout, or up to eight abreast in high density short haul. A double lobe fuselage section was considered with stowage under the cabin floor for standard LD-1 and LD-3 containers.

Where ranges of over 5,000 nautical miles (9,262km) were required on the long thin routes, a 200-seater was being considered with four 26,700lb (119kN) thrust JT10D engines being shoulder mounted to assist with noise reduction. However, this engine configuration suffered from structural and aerodynamic complications, and by 1974 a return had been made to more conventional underwing podded engines, with two and three engine variants being considered.

To determine a series of common configurations, Boeing contacted between 30 and 40 airlines including the major US domestic and European operators. United Airlines undertook to collect and analyse the data, and remained active in the overall definition of the Boeing 767 until it was launched, when they became the first customer. However no common thread could be found throughout the mid-1970s on which to define

ABOVE: The Boeing Narrow Bodied Plant at Renton is on the shores of Lake Washington. The latest development, the stretched 757-300ER was formally rolled out on 31 May 1998. *Boeing*

the aircraft. In concept form the 7X7 was proposed as a wide-body twin-aisle airliner for medium or long range, the underwing engines in pods, while the three engine version located the third engine in the rear fuselage. The position of the tailplane varied from a high T-tail configuration to one mounted low on the fuselage. The wing was expected to use the current advanced aft-loaded supercritical aerodynamics, giving low drag and fuel efficiency, as well as a lighter structure and additional fuel capacity. Amongst the variables still current were the size of the cabin, in both width and length, the payload/range requirements and the selection of power plants.

At the Paris Show in June 1975 a model of the 7X7 shown jointly by Boeing and Aeritalia had three engines and featured a low set tailplane. With the demise of so many other commercial projects due to the difficult economic conditions, Boeing was criticised for not making greater use of existing technology and adapting existing airframes, although Boeing was also studying the 727-300 stretch which was revealed in early 1974.

The launch of a completely new design in a period of high inflation results in the costs becoming increasingly more difficult to recover. In order to overcome the inflationary headwind, the new project would need to combine low cost engineering including the use of composite materials and efficient aerodynamics, power plants and systems to reduce fuel consumption and noise while increasing overall efficiency. Boeing were considering producing initially a medium range aircraft, which if sold in sufficient numbers would finance the launch of a long range version two years further on. Two fuselage lengths were being considered carrying from 175 to 201 passengers, with a high-density inclusive-tour layout capable of packing in up to 283 passengers. At least the fuselage width had been set at 198in (5m) allowing a twin aisle seating layout, and being about two thirds of the size of the wide bodied Trijets, the 7X7 would be complementary rather than competitive with them. Five power plant options, both in type and configuration were still open, and three different range capabilities. The range options varied from 2,160nm (4,000km) for the European carriers, 2,700nm miles (5,000km) for the US domestic trunk routes and over 4,860nm (9,000km) for the intercontinental operations. Further cost savings would be achieved by making the cockpit capable of a two-crew operation, facilitated by installing an integrated digital flight control and navigation system, combined with cathode-ray tube (CRT) information displays, replacing the old analogue instruments. This would create greater reliability and reduce cockpit work load.

By the 1980s a 6-7 percent growth was predicted for worldwide air transport, with an increase in extended range non stop routes. Combining this conservative growth, with the demands for greater fuel efficiency and reduced noise, requiring replacement of the first and second generation jet airliners, Boeing predicted a market for some 1,500 airliners in the 7X7 category, of which they expected to capture a share of 1,000 aircraft over a period of 15 years, half of which would be to the domestic US trunk airlines. These US trunk operators were essential to the commercial success of the programme, and the launch was to be based on a common requirement from two US airlines and an export sale, most likely to Europe. Once the decision to go ahead was made, a four year development programme was planned with initial deliveries due by early 1981, depending on the launch decision. Even as a project the Boeing 7X7 was an international programme with Italian Government investing $230 million in new production facilities for 7X7 major components, Aeritalia having a 20 percent risk share in the programme, designing and testing hardware and working as part of the overall team of 400 engineers on detailed aerodynamics.

In June 1976 the layout had evolved into a low tailplane configuration with very high aspect ratio wings and a double lobe fuselage with the width increased to 210in (5.3m), allowing an eight-abreast twin aisle layout for up to 200 passengers. In this form it was known as the 7X7-962 and would be capable of carrying 20 first class and 180 tourist class passengers up to 2,346nm (4,345km). The competing 7X7-963 trijet was being studied by a completely different team of engineers. The twin was favoured for reduced maintenance costs, but the engines would require greater installed power to overcome the engine failure case, reducing economy.

To reduce weight and maintenance, composite materials were to be used in the cabin floor panels, wing leading edges, inboard ailerons, elevators, parts of the flaps, the centre engine duct for the trijet, and many other components including non structural fairings. Other weight-saving structural

ABOVE LEFT: The wide body facility at Everett alongside Paine Field was built by Boeing for the production of the Boeing 747 Jumbo Jet, the largest airliner in the world. The launch order for the Boeing 747 was placed by PanAm, and PanAm 747-100 N747PA was the second aircraft built and the first for the airline. This aircraft is seen at London Heathrow in August 1990. *Philip Birtles*

LEFT: The latest development of the Boeing 747 is the -400, the main recognition point being wing-tip upswept winglets. A total of 1,305 747s have been sold, with 1,159 delivered by the end of July 1998. Korean 747-400 HL7483 is seen on final approach to Hong Kong Kai Tak in April 1998. *Philip Birtles*

advances included stringerless sidewall panels, titanium centre-section structure and carbon brakes. The use of digital avionics and computers on the flightdeck would also reduce weight while improving performance and giving higher reliability. Every 100lb (45kg) of weight saved, was estimated to be worth 50nm (93km) extra range for a given payload. Economy would be enhanced by using a digital auto throttle throughout the flight.

Between mid-1976 and the spring of 1977 the configuration changed again, the 7X7 being joined by the smaller 7N7, and both having T-tails, as shown in model form at the Paris Show that June. The 7X7 had now become a trijet, with the narrow body 7N7 powered by two engines. The larger aircraft carried only 20 more passengers, but the major differences were range, freight capacity, and the over water capability which was restricted with the twin.

A launch had been hoped for in October 1977, but the prospective US initial airlines were unable to agree on the fuselage width and the number of engines. To attempt to overcome the problem, Boeing reverted to the earlier 198in (5m) wide fuselage, with the twin-jet launched first, followed later by the trijet. On 5 January 1978 Boeing confirmed its commitment to producing a new family of airliners by announcing plans for a major extension of the manufacturing facility at Everett, which had originally been built 10 years earlier for production of the

ABOVE: The latest aircraft to be built at Everett is the 777, which required the building of two new production bays for final assembly. The latest version is the 777-300 seen on roll-out at Everett, having been launched into development by an order from Cathay Pacific. Following the flight development programme, the Rolls-Royce Trent powered 777-300 was refurbished and delivered to Cathay. *Boeing*

Boeing 747 Jumbo Jet. In the middle of February Boeing announced the designations of 757, 767 and 777 to a family of new and derivative airliner projects, the aim being to define firm specifications in time for a product launch around mid-1978.

These new projects consisted of a narrow body twin-jet derivative of the previously proposed 727-300 seating 150 to 170 passengers; the 767-100 twin all new semi wide body with seven abreast layout fitting an American Airlines requirement for carrying 175 passengers over 2,000nm (3,704km); the two seat row longer 767-200 fitting a United requirement for carrying 190 passengers over the same range; the 777-100 transcontinental trijet carrying 175 passengers up to 2,700nm (5,000km); and the 777-200 with an oceanic range of 4,500nm (8,334km), a little less than the 5,000nm (9,260km) more than the big trijets.

The wings, tail components, flightdeck and cabin section were to be common to all members of the 767/777 family, the go ahead of both 757 and 767/777 programmes being targeted

LEFT: On the flight line at Everett in May 1998 with one of the paint buildings in the background, is a production 777-300 for Cathay Pacific being prepared for flight. *Philip Birtles*

BELOW LEFT: Emirates 777-200ER A6-EMD on final approach to Hong Kong Kai Tak in April 1998, the third of the Boeing wide body jet airliners to be produced at Everett. Total orders for the Boeing 777 stand at 392, with 146 delivered by the end of July 1998. *Philip Birtles*

aisle layout, the underfloor cargo hold could only take one standard LD-3 container, not two across as with the Airbus. Boeing therefore proposed LD-3A containers which would fit side by side with the LD-3s. The 777 was still planned to follow on about two years behind.

With the expansion of the Everett facility to accommodate the new aircraft, total wide-bodied airliner production would be 200 aircraft annually, employing 12,000 people over the seven-year build up. The combined 767/777 lines would start at two aircraft per month for the first two years and the market was seen as 1,500 767s and 777-100s worth $32,000 million, plus another 300 to 400 777-200s worth another $10,000 million. The total investment was around $1,500 million by 1986, financed internally with additional investment from Italy, and possibly Japan.

On 14 July 1978 came the long awaited decision when United placed the launch order worth $1,200 million for 30 767-200s for entry into service in mid-1982, some 12 years after the initial studies commenced. There had been strong competition from the Airbus A310, but United made their decision six weeks earlier than expected, specifying a 198in (5m) wide twin lobe cabin capable of carrying up to 197 passengers. The aircraft had a low set tailplane, a configuration which was settled at the last minute, and power was to come from a pair of P&W JT9D-7R engines developing 44,300lb (197kN) thrust, similar to the engines used in their 747s. The range of 2,200nm (4,074km) was ideal for the United transcontinental routes, and the underfloor hold was reconfigured to take 22 LD-2 containers with room for bulk cargo.

for the end of 1978. To overcome the economic risks of starting the two programmes unaided, international collaboration was sought, with Aeritalia transferring their 7X7 work and investment to the 767/777 programme, and additional support from Japan being encouraged. The choice of engines was still to be made. The 767 was beginning to emerge as a shorter range aircraft, but with the common wing policy had more wing area than optimum to cope with the higher gross weights of the proposed 777. This did allow a much simplified range of high lift devices on the leading and trailing edges.

By May 1978 the 767-200 was given priority due to a firm interest by United Airlines and the choice between three proven engines. Design work was progressing particularly on the wing with over 67 different wind tunnel models being tested, and the cabin with the seven-abreast layout gave room for 150 to 250 seats without the fuselage being structurally too long or aerodynamically too short. Although this gave a twin-

Meanwhile the 777 trijet was quietly shelved, to re-emerge later as an all-new big twin-jet airliner, and all the earlier extended range requirements were achieved by developments of the basic 767 airframe.

# 2 DESIGN AND DEVELOPMENT

Although the Boeing 767 had a mainly traditional structure, major advances were made with new materials, particularly the latest aluminium alloys giving improved strength and corrosion resistance. Composite materials were used in a number of secondary and non-load bearing structures which gave a weight saving of around 1,000lb (454kg) over the use of light alloys for the same items, and therefore increasing payload. The principal composite material used was du Pont Kevlar graphite/epoxy used in the construction of the ailerons, elevators, rudder, spoilers, undercarriage doors, wing fixed leading and trailing edge fairings, engine cowling skins and wing to fuselage fairings. Nomex honeycomb panels were used in some high structural and corrosion prone areas such as the cabin floor panels. Computer-aided design (CAD) was used extensively providing the design parameters for the production tooling achieving cost effective manufacture.

One of the longest lead items on any aircraft are the main forgings for the undercarriage structure, the massive load carrying shock struts for the main leg consisting of one piece forgings in vacuum melted steel. The tooling for these critical forgings had to be placed some months before the launch of the aircraft to keep delays to a minimum.

To maintain cost effective efficiency the 767 used the latest supercritical wing technology with the 22 percent thicker aft loaded section developing more lift for less drag. This gave an lighter and simpler wing structure with less sweep back and an increased fuel capacity for longer range. Control was achieved by a complex range of devices mounted on the wing box, consisting of hydraulically controlled outboard low-speed ailerons, inboard high speed ailerons which droop with the flaps to keep the nose lower on the approach for better view, leading and trailing edge flaps and electrically operated flight and ground lift dump spoilers. The leading edge slats are built in six sections and can be set in various positions in relation to the trailing edge flaps for optimum performance during take-off and

BELOW: When the first 767 was rolled out at Everett on 4 August 1981 a crowd of 15,000 spectators were there to welcome it, the programme having been launched by the order from United Airlines for 30 aircraft in July 1978. *Boeing*

landing. The conventional single slotted flaps occupy the entire trailing edge of the wing not covered by the ailerons. Conventional rudder and elevators were fitted to the swept back tail surfaces.

Many hours were spent proving the design in the wind tunnel with well over 26,000 hours accumulated, (compared with 14,000 hours for the 747, and only 4,000 hours for the 727). However, the demands for greater efficiency required careful refinement of the design to achieve the competitive performance for the new aircraft. Structural testing was also an important part of the design programme, a complete static test airframe being tested in three phases, the first of which was to determine the ability of the 767 to carry the normal design loads. Stage two covered loading on the airframe to represent growth development, and the testing culminating in a combination of the worst design cases which resulted in the final destruction of the airframe.

In addition to the complete airframe structure, slats and flaps were tested to destruction and the undercarriage back-up structure was carefully inspected. From April 1982 fatigue testing commenced on a primary structure airframe consisting of the wing, fuselage and fin, supported by component trials, the plan to complete 25,000 cycles by the time of certification, and keeping well ahead of service flying. By March 1983 the static test airframe had achieved the equivalent of 20 years flying, while at the same time the fatigue specimen had simulated 50,000 flights. By November 1983 when 18 months of structural testing of the airframe had been achieved, the use of the new processes and materials in the 767 had been proven. The fatigue test airframe finally completed the equivalent of 100,000 flight cycles, which was equivalent to about 40 years airline service, and structural modifications were found to be minimal.

ABOVE: The Boeing owned 767 prototype N767BA made its maiden flight from Everett on 26 September 1981, and was later joined in the flight development programme by the first three aircraft for United Airlines to achieve FAA certification in August 1982. *Boeing*

RIGHT: The 767 prototype N767BA was later extensively modified as an airborne surveillance test-bed (AST). The aircraft is a key element of the US Department of Defence Ballistic Missile Defence Organisation and is a technology demonstration programme based at Boeing Field to support development and evaluation of defensive systems to counter intercontinental and theatre ballistic missiles. The large cupola on top of the fuselage houses infra red sensors to detect the aerodynamic heating of incoming missiles and is sensitive enough to detect the heat of a human body at a distance of more than 1,000 miles (1,852km) against the cold background of space. The aircraft normally carries a crew of 15 on missions lasting up to eight hours, flying at altitudes of above 42,000ft (12,802m). *Boeing*

The first 767, N767BA, the company-owned development Pratt & Whitney JT9D-7R4-powered prototype was rolled out at Everett on 4 August 1981 when preparations continued towards the maiden flight on 26 September 1981, starting a very demanding and intensive flight development programme involving six aircraft. Tom Edmunds, the 767 Project test pilot, climbed the 767 away from the runway at Paine Field three days earlier than planned when the programme was launched three years previously. The take-off roll used 3,000ft (914m) with a gross weight of 240,000lb (108,862kg) and during the 2 hour 4 minute sortie, handling characteristics were checked from the stall buffet boundary of 102kt up to 225kt. Flap operation was checked to the 30-degree setting for landing, and the undercarriage and speed brake operation were checked with flaps both up and down. The aircraft behaved exactly as expected, and the crew were particularly enthusiastic about the digital flight instruments and CRTs for the clarity and the ability to provide continuous precise orientation.

Following the initial testing at Paine Field, the first 767 was flown to the Flight Development centre at Boeing Field where the bulk of the flight testing was undertaken. The first aircraft was allocated to airworthiness, control and stability, and aerodynamic performance, with flutter testing being completed in about 15 flying hours. The 767 reached Mach 0.91 and 43,100ft (13,137m), the early flight trials covering longitudinal stability and control, buffet boundaries, dynamic damping and the approach to the stall in different configurations. During early December, the first aircraft was based at Palmdale in California giving access to the very long runways at Edwards Air Force Base where minimum unstick velocity test and other critical trials such as the maximum energy brake test could be made.

The second 767 joined the development programme with the first flight on 4 November and was allocated to testing of the controls, the digital avionics, engines and the electrical systems. The third 767 was used to survey flight loads, test the pneumatic and automatic flight controls, and examine in more detail the stall and buffet characteristics. The fourth aircraft was used for aerodynamic measurements and noise investigation, while the fifth aircraft, the first for Delta determined performance with the GE engine. The total certification programme of 1,600 flying hours, including an additional 185 flying hours due to the fundamental change from three to two crew was completed over a period of 10 months by 30 July 1982, a deadline set in December 1978.

Following the Boeing-owned first development, the remaining aircraft in the development programme were destined for delivery to the initial customers after being refurbished. The second aircraft — VA002 — was used for the FAA evaluation starting on 10 December 1981, with VA003 making its first flight on 28 December; VA004 first flew two days later. All three of these production aircraft were destined for United and were powered by a pair of P&W JT9D-7R4 engines. The first four P&W-powered 767s flew 1,445 hours in 1,251 sorties up to the end of June 1982 and a further 239 hours were flown in 230 sorties by the GE-powered VA301 which joined the flight development programme on 19 February 1982. This aircraft started the certification flying in March with full clearance achieved in six months. As well as all the normal systems, aerodynamic and performance testing of the new aircraft, the innovation of the digital cockpit controls had to be proven in operation.

Following the favourable findings of a US Presidential task force confirming the safety of the two-crew operation, 16 of the first 17 customers changed to the two-crew flightdeck, VA006 being moved immediately to the modification line after the roll-out on 16 January 1982, to be converted for two-crew operation. With the modifications complete it joined the flight test programme on 27 May before leaving Seattle on 6 July for a

demanding 15-day 29,000-mile (53,708km) FAA monitored functional and reliability (F&R) tour. During this programme seven countries were visited around Europe and the Middle East, when it was possible to combine the testing with demonstrations to prospective airline customers. In 43 flights taking a total of 81 hours flying time, more than 1,300 passengers were carried from airlines, governments, industry and the media. This was the seventh 767 off the production line for later delivery to United and the return flight from Oslo to Seattle established a new non-stop distance record for a twin-jet airliner. The flight of 4,333nm (8,025km) was made in an elapsed time of 9hr 50min at an average speed of 507mph (816kph), and on arrival 12,800lb (5,806kg) of fuel remained in the tanks.

The flight development results consistently demonstrated better performance than originally predicted, the most significant areas being lower drag and reduced empty weight. Significant improvements were found with airfield performance, altitude capability and fuel consumption, giving better range. The flying characteristics resembled a large 737 and was free from the feeling of bulk associated with larger aircraft like the Boeing 747. The late decision to change to a two-crew cockpit presented a major challenge to Boeing, as the first 30 aircraft had to be modified without delays to the delivery schedule. However, this change did bring commonality with the 757 flightdeck and crew operation. The 767 was certificated to an initial take-off weight of 300,000lb (136,077kg) by which time 24 767s had been completed and were being modified for two crew, to meet a delivery schedule of 25 aircraft to seven airlines by the end of 1982. Approval was given by the FAA for a common type approval for the 757 and 767 on 22 July 1983 despite fundamental differences between the aerodynamics of the two aircraft.

BELOW: The first major development of the 767 was the stretched 767-300 launched into development by an initial order from Japan Airlines on 29 September 1983. The cabin length was increased by 21ft 1in (6.43m) allowing 50 more passengers to be carried. *Boeing*

# 3 PRODUCTION

To spread the financial load, the 767 was always planned as an international risk-sharing programme. The Boeing contribution was to be 53 percent by value of the first 200 aircraft consisting of the wing, nose section including the flightdeck, cabin floor and engine nacelles. Major overseas risk shares were taken by Aeritalia and the Japanese Commercial Transport Development Corporation (CTDC) with over 100 staff from each organisation trained by Boeing before participating in the appropriate detail design and manufacture in their own organisations.

The Japanese CTDC is a consortium of Fuji, Kawasaki and Mitsubishi with the group taking responsibility for the design and production of fuselage panels, entry doors, composite wing to fuselage fairings, main undercarriage doors and the wing ribs between the front and rear spars. In addition Kawasaki produce the wing flap gear boxes and Teijin Seiki are responsible for the

wing spoiler actuators, in both cases as sub contractors. Aeritalia have design and production responsibility for the control surfaces including trailing edge flaps, leading edge slats, wingtips, elevators, rudder and radome. The remaining 767 major suppliers are North American based.

Italy used the 767 programme to develop their expertise and technology in the manufacture of major structural components using composites. These Aeritalia produced advanced composite structures cover some 30 percent of the 767 external surfaces, and include the largest carbon fibre components produced for a commercial aircraft at that time. It was Aeritalia's first involvement in a commercial risk sharing venture, and by the time the flight development programme had commenced, the Italian Government had invested over $94 million in the

BELOW: The Boeing 767 made use of a range of advanced composites, particularly with the control surfaces. *Boeing*

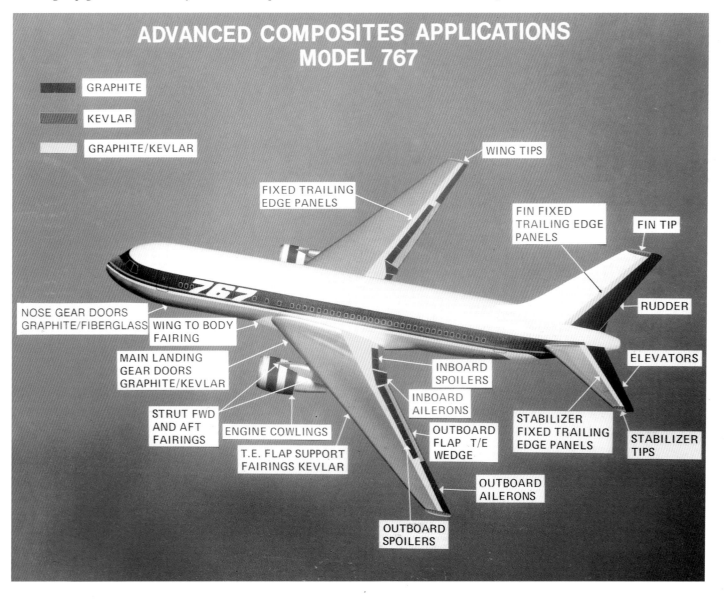

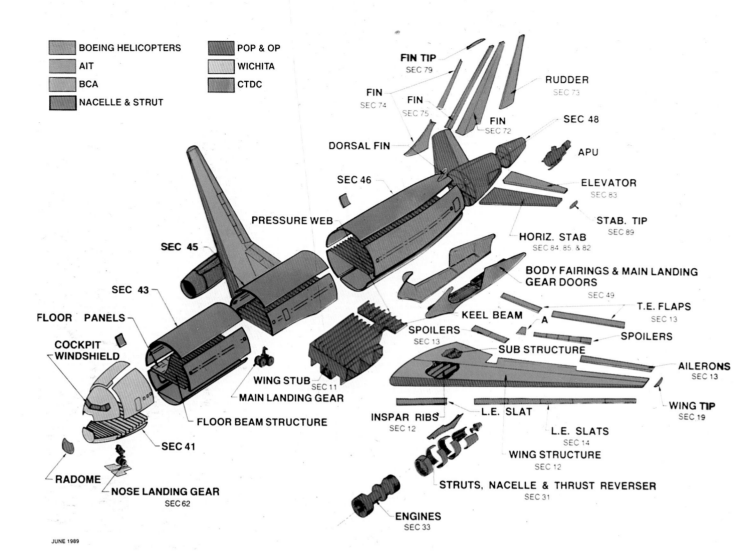

**LEGEND:**
- BOEING HELICOPTERS
- AIT
- BCA
- NACELLE & STRUT
- POP & OP
- WICHITA
- CTDC

FIN TIP
SEC 79

RUDDER
SEC 73

FIN
SEC 74

FIN
SEC 75

FIN
SEC 72

SEC 48

DORSAL FIN

APU

SEC 46

ELEVATOR
SEC 83

PRESSURE WEB

STAB. TIP
SEC 89

SEC 45

HORIZ. STAB
SEC 84, 85 & 82

SEC 43

BODY FAIRINGS & MAIN LANDING
GEAR DOORS
SEC 49

FLOOR PANELS

KEEL BEAM
A

T.E. FLAPS
SEC 13

COCKPIT
WINDSHIELD

SPOILERS
SEC 13

SPOILERS

SUB STRUCTURE

WING STUB
SEC 11

AILERONS
SEC 13

MAIN LANDING GEAR

FLOOR BEAM STRUCTURE

INSPAR RIBS
SEC 12

L.E. SLAT

WING TIP
SEC 19

SEC 41

L.E. SLATS
SEC 14

RADOME

WING STRUCTURE
SEC 12

NOSE LANDING GEAR
SEC 62

STRUTS, NACELLE & THRUST REVERSER
SEC 31

ENGINES
SEC 33

JUNE 1989

programme. Not only did the programme help regenerate the Italian aerospace industry, but it provided an accelerated impetus for an upgrade of the technological capability, and the Boeing stringent quality standards taught new disciplines making the company more competitive in world markets.

At the launch of the 767 programme, Aeritalia had planned to be producing 8.5 sets of components per month by the time the aircraft entered service, each set being valued at $1.2 million at 1982 levels, representing 12.5 percent of the total value of the airframe. When Aeritalia committed to becoming a risk sharing partner in the 767 programme on 14 August 1978 they agreed to provide for a capacity of up to 12.5 ship sets per month, and break even was anticipated on delivery of the 501st set of assemblies.

However, with the poor world economy in the early 1980s the demand for new airliners was reduced and the initial production plans had to be cut back, delaying the break-even point and return on investment. The early optimism generated by the launch order was reduced by the lack of significant follow on orders, and some deferrals of deliveries. Despite this, confidence in the overall success, assisted by the planned longer range developments never faltered.

ABOVE: The Boeing 767 is a truly international programme with risk sharing partners in Japan and Italy, as well as the USA. Apart from the Rolls-Royce RB211 engines, the Pop & Op items come from North America. The AIT parts of the programme are built in Italy, and the CTDC blue fuselage sections are supplied from Japan. *Boeing*

TOP RIGHT: The construction of the 767 starts with forward cabin sections being assembled in the vast building at Everett. The fuselage sections and the wings are brought together on the assembly site for structural joining, before moving forward on its undercarriage to the equipping area where the engines are also fitted. *Boeing*

RIGHT: Boeing 767-200s and 767-300s are produced side by side on the same assembly line with a second identical sized bay next door to accommodate any additional capacity. Boeing 767-346 JA8234 — the first for Japan Air Lines — is close to completion with the engines fitted, and is in front of an Air New Zealand 767-200 and the second 767-346 for JAL, the 150th 767 to be built. *Boeing*

# 4 TECHNICAL SPECIFICATION

| TYPE | 767-200ER | 767-300ER | 767-300 FREIGHTER | 767-400ER |
|---|---|---|---|---|
| Wing span | 156ft 1in (47.6m) | 156ft 1in (47.6m) | 156ft 1in (47.6m) | 79ft 1½in (54.6m) |
| Length | 159ft 2in (48.5m) | 180ft 3in (54.9m) | 180ft 3in (54.9m) | 201ft 5in (61.4m) |
| Height | 52ft (15.8m) | 52ft (15.8m) | 52ft (15.8m) | 55ft 1½in (16.8m) |
| Wing Area | 3,052sq ft (283.5sq m) | 3,052sq ft (283.5sq m) | 3,052sq ft (283.5sq m) | — |
| Pax 2-class | 224 | 269 | — | 304 |
| Pax 3-class | 181 | 218 | — | 245 |
| Max t/o wt | 395,000lb (179,545kg) | 412,000lb (187,273kg) | 412,000lb (187,273kg) | 450,000lb (204,120kg) |
| Max landing wt | 285,000lb (129,545kg) | 320,000lb (145,455kg) | 326,000lb (148,182kg) | — |
| Zero fuel wt | 260,000lb (118,182kg) | 295,000lb (134,091kg) | 309,000lb (140,455kg) | 228,900lb (103,830kg) |
| Max Fuel | 24,140 US gal (91,400lt) | 24,140 US gal (91,400lt) | 24,140 US gal (91,400lt) | 24,140 US gal (91,400lt) |
| Cargo vol, lower hold | bulk 3,930cu ft (111cu m) | bulk 5,266cu ft (149cu m) | | bulk 4,908cu ft (139 cu m) |
| | LD-2 3,070cu ft (87cu m) | LD-2 4,030cu ft (114cu m) | LD-2 3,720cu ft (93cu m) | LD-2 5,057cu ft (000cu m) |
| Cargo vol, main deck | — | — | 11,990cu ft (340cu m) | — |
| Engines | | | | |
| P&W | PW4056 | PW4060 | PW4060/4062 | PW4000 |
| thrust | 57,100lb (254kN) | 60,250lb (268kN) | 60,250lb (268kN) | 69,242lb (308kN) |
| GE | CF6-80C2 | CF6-80C2 | CF6-80C2B6F | CF6-80C2 |
| thrust | 56,430lb (251kN) | 56,430lb (251kN) | 56,430lb (251kN) | 56,430lb (251kN) |
| R-R | — | RB211-524G/H | RB211-524H | — |
| thrust | | 59,350lb (264kN) | 59,350lb (264kN) | |

RIGHT: The main undercarriage consists of a four wheel bogie with a door fairing covering the leg when it is retracted sideways. *Philip Birtles*

BELOW RIGHT: As the main undercarriage units retract sideways, a fuselage mounted door opens to allow the wheels to tuck in, and then closes behind the wheels. *Philip Birtles*

BELOW: The nose undercarriage consists of a forward retracting twin wheel unit, the front doors normally remaining closed apart from during the retraction and lowering sequence. *Philip Birtles*

BOTTOM LEFT: The structure of the Boeing 767 is mainly traditional with toilets located in the mid cabin and galleys at each end. The wide body cabin allows a typical economy layout of seven abreast seating, and there is adequate room for containerised cargo and baggage under the cabin floor. *Boeing*

## UNDERCARRIAGE

The two main undercarriage units carry a typical Boeing four-wheel bogie which retracts inwards to lie in the fuselage between the air conditioning bay and rear freight hold. The nose undercarriage is a twin-wheel steerable unit controlled by either pilot which retracts forward. Retraction is achieved hydraulically and upward lock is achieved by the gear doors. In an emergency the undercarriage can be lowered by gravity.

## POWER SYSTEMS

The aircraft controls and undercarriage obtained their primary power from three independent hydraulic systems, two of which were operated by engine pumps plus electric pumps, and the third was powered by two electric pumps and an air driven pump running off the auxiliary power unit (APU). Emergency power for the primary flight controls, flaps and slats, tailplane incidence trim, landing gear operation, nose wheel steering and wheel brakes is provided by a pair of transformer rectifiers powered by a nickel cadmium battery.

## FLIGHTDECK

The 767 was planned from the start to be operated by a crew of two, but provision was made for a three-crew cockpit in case of difficulties with safety aspects and union manning demands.

The spacious flightdeck was laid out to provide the latest comfort and efficiency standards using modern digital technology in the information displays. The traditional analogue instruments were replaced by three cathode ray tube (CRT) display panels, one providing primary flight information replacing the altitude indicator; the second for horizontal situation indication, which can also be used for compass information and weather radar; and the third display which provides information for the central caution and warn-

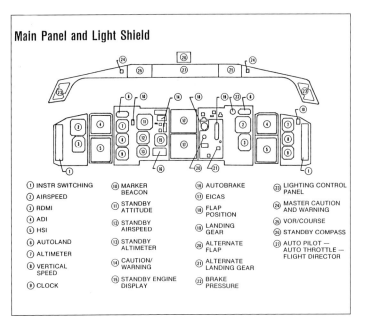

## Main Panel and Light Shield

1. INSTR SWITCHING
2. AIRSPEED
3. RDMI
4. ADI
5. HSI
6. AUTOLAND
7. ALTIMETER
8. VERTICAL SPEED
9. CLOCK
10. MARKER BEACON
11. STANDBY ATTITUDE
12. STANDBY AIRSPEED
13. STANDBY ALTIMETER
14. CAUTION/WARNING
15. STANDBY ENGINE DISPLAY
16. AUTOBRAKE
17. EICAS
18. FLAP POSITION
19. LANDING GEAR
20. ALTERNATE FLAP
21. ALTERNATE LANDING GEAR
22. BRAKE PRESSURE
23. LIGHTING CONTROL PANEL
24. MASTER CAUTION AND WARNING
25. VOR/COURSE
26. STANDBY COMPASS
27. AUTO PILOT — AUTO THROTTLE — FLIGHT DIRECTOR

FAR LEFT: When the APU is running a small door opens on the top of the fuselage at the base of the fin as an air intake. *Philip Birtles*

LEFT: The auxiliary power unit (APU) is located in the tail cone and exhausts to the rear. The unit provides power to the aircraft systems when the main engines are shut down, and can also be used for main engine starting at remote locations. *Philip Birtles*

LEFT: The two-crew advanced flightdeck gives a good view and weather radar is housed under a nose mounted radome. *Philip Birtles*

ABOVE: The two-crew flightdeck of the 767 is identical to the 757, allowing crews to be licensed for both types without additional conversion training. The cathode ray tube (CRT) main instruments include the Attitude Director Indicator (duplicated in front of each pilot), above the Horizontal Situation Indicator, both of which provide the crew with flight operations information. In the centre are vertical paired EICAS, or Engine Indication and Crew Alerting System CRTs which also provide systems data. *Boeing*

BELOW: The flightdeck in the photo is of 767-222ER N605UA which was the seventh off the line, and the fifth to be delivered to United Airlines. *Boeing*

ing system. Through the associated computers, these displays only provide the information needed for the particular phase of flight reducing significantly the crew workload. The displays also show the crew check list electronically, each stage having to be actioned before moving on to the next item. The Sperry produced automatic flight management system (FMS) allows the crew to achieve a more accurate utilisation of the aircraft as well as achieving automatic landings to Cat 3B standard. The FMS has a dual CRT display panel and keyboard mounted on the centre console between the two pilots, just forward of the throttles, or thrust levers, as they are now known. Above this on the main instrument panel is the central warning panel, the importance of any warnings being indicated as red for urgent, amber for precaution and green for information. All the information displayed on the flat screens is bright enough to be seen clearly even in the strongest sunlight, without dazzling the crew at night.

## CONTROL SURFACES

Control was achieved by a complex range of devices mounted on the wing box, consisting of hydraulically controlled outboard low-speed ailerons, inboard high speed ailerons which droop with the flaps to keep the nose lower on the approach for better view, leading and trailing edge flaps and electrically operated flight and ground lift dump spoilers. The leading edge slats are built in six sections and can be set in various positions

ABOVE: A typical Business Class interior of the Boeing 767 with six abreast seating.

BELOW: The Boeing 767 wing features high lift devices on the leading edge consisting of retractable slats, and trailing edge flaps with the engines hanging from pylons. *Philip Birtles*

BELOW LEFT: The wing trailing edge flaps are operated by screw jacks running along flap tracks located in underwing fairings. *Philip Birtles*

ABOVE: Just outboard of the inner flap track is an inboard aileron. Beyond that are the outboard flaps and near the wingtip are the outboard ailerons. *Philip Birtles*

ABOVE RIGHT: The Leisure-operated 767-39HER is powered by a pair of General Electric CF6-80C2 high by-pass engines. *Philip Birtles*

RIGHT: A comparison of the overall diameter of the CF6-80C2 engine with the size of the exhaust gives some indication of the amount of by-pass which gives greater economy and quieter operation. *Philip Birtles*

BELOW RIGHT: The GE CF6-80C2 engines are mounted on a pylon well ahead of the wing leading edge. *Philip Birtles*

BELOW LEFT: The wing to fuselage joint is faired to create the least amount of drag and a landing light is mounted in the wing root. *Philip Birtles*

in relation to the trailing edge flaps for optimum performance during take-off and landing. The conventional single slotted flaps occupy the entire trailing edge of the wing not covered by the ailerons. Conventional rudder and elevators were fitted to the swept back tail surfaces.

## ENGINES

The 767 offers three main engine manufacturers — Pratt & Whitney; General Electric's CF6-80A; and the Rolls-Royce RB211. United's launch order for 30 767s selected 44,300lb (197kN)-thrust P&W JT9D-7Rs, derated from the engines used on the United 747s, after a hard fought contest with GE. FAA certification of the Pratt & Whitney-powered 767s was achieved on 30 July 1982 and P&W's JT9D-7R4s were used by 10 of the first 17 aircraft off the production line.

The first GE-powered 767 was for Delta and it commenced its flight development programme in February 1982 flying 315 hours on engine certification. FAA certification of the CF6-80A-powered 767 was awarded in early October, clearing the way for delivery to the launch customers of both Delta and American Airlines.

With both the P&W and GE engines powering the 767, in March 1987 an agreement was reached between Boeing and Rolls-Royce to consider fitting the 60,600lb (270kN) thrust RB524-D4D engines to the 767. As a result BA placed an order in August 1987 for 11 767-300s with options on a further

15 worth $500 million, the engines being similar to those powering the BA 747-400s. The first Rolls-Royce RB211-524G-powered 767-300 was rolled out at Everett in April 1989, commencing the flight test programme on 23 May. CAA clearance was achieved in July and full certification of the 60,600lb (270kN) thrust 524H engine was awarded in November ready for delivery to BA. The story of ETOPS/EROPS is covered in the next chapter.

the -200ER for extended range, giving a useful transatlantic capability for the less dense routes. By the 1990s Boeing planned for the 767s to have a 6,000nm (11,112km) range, bringing the challenges of flying twin-engine aircraft over the major oceanic routes. To achieve this desired unlimited over-water capability a long way from diversionary airfields, engine reliability and systems redundancy was improved, with back up from the APU.

## 767-200 AND 200ER

To help attract further sales but at a minimum cost the basic 767-200 had fuel located in the wing centre section becoming

## 767-300 AND 300ER

The next major development was the 767-300 which was first ordered by Japan Airlines on 29 September 1983. This version

ABOVE: The first user of the RB211-524G/H on the 767, BA and Rolls-Royce worked with the CAA to achieve 120min EROPS approval in 1991. As this engine was already fitted to the BA 747-200s, reliability figures had already been established. BA then used the 767-300ERs for the less busy transatlantic routes. Photo shows 767-336ER G-BNWD *City of Copenhagen* on finals. *Philip Birtles*

LEFT: A retractable tail skid is fitted to the 767 to protect the rear fuselage against ground strike during over rotation. *Philip Birtles*

INSET, RIGHT: On the port side of the fuselage, just forward of the rear passenger door, is an inward opening door hold for bulky loose items such as golf clubs and skis, as well as the crew baggage. *Philip Birtles*

ABOVE RIGHT: The forward cargo hold has a large upward opening door for access to the palletised freight. *Philip Birtles*

FAR RIGHT: The rear underfloor cargo hold has an upward opening door about half the size of the front hold. Behind and above is the rear service door for catering access. *Philip Birtles*

RIGHT: Air Aruba leased 767-204ER G-BYAA from Britannia Airways, and it is seen landing at Luton in their colours with the reverse thrust deployed in April 1992. It has also carried the Dutch registration PH-AHM. *Philip Birtles*

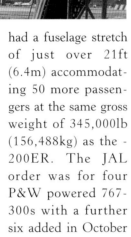

had a fuselage stretch of just over 21ft (6.4m) accommodating 50 more passengers at the same gross weight of 345,000lb (156,488kg) as the -200ER. The JAL order was for four P&W powered 767-300s with a further six added in October 1986. The first 767-300 made its maiden flight on 30 January 1986 and certification was completed on 25 September after 430 hours of flight testing.

The next logical development was to produce the 767-300ER with additional fuel in the wings, some structural strengthening and power coming from the newer generation 60,000lb (0000kg) thrust GE CF6-80C2 or P&W PW4056 with nacelles common to the 747-400. The initial gross weight was 380,000lb (172,364kg), giving a similar range to the 767-200ER, but with a further weight increase to 400,000lb (181,436kg) an additional 500 miles (926km) range was achieved. The new engines gave the 767-300ER a 5 percent improvement in economy over the basic -300.

A typical turnaround at London Gatwick of Leisure International 767-39HER G-UKLI, one of two on lease from ILFC. *All photos Philip Birtles*

MAIN PICTURE: The aircraft approaches the stand.

BOTTOM: The GE CF6-80C2 engines are ready to be switched off at the end of the flight.

RIGHT: Ground power is plugged in as soon as the aircraft comes to a halt to keep the systems live, and avoiding the continual running of the APU.

BOTTOM RIGHT: Steps are pushed up to the forward door while the crew undertake their arrival checks and report any snags to the engineers.

ABOVE: The passengers exit the aircraft on to a damp Gatwick apron after the return from Orlando.

BOTTOM: Meanwhile at the rear end of the aircraft, the rear galleys are being cleared leaving room for the passenger baggage to be unloaded.

ABOVE: On the opposite side from the passenger doors, the catering service vehicle unloads the discarded catering units from the forward service door.

BOTTOM: The passenger baggage is packed in containers for easier mechanical handling.

MAIN PICTURE: Once removed from the aircraft, the baggage containers are lowered to ground level and manoeuvred onto roller-equipped trolleys.

BELOW: Once all the baggage containers are unloaded, they are towed in a train to the baggage hall.

BOTTOM: As the baggage is towed away, the engineers commence the turnaround inspection of the aircraft and engines. This work is contracted to BA engineers.

BOTTOM RIGHT AND OPPOSITE PAGE, TOP LEFT: An hydraulic lifting platform is positioned by the forward hold ready to unload the cargo — less urgent than the baggage for the waiting passengers but a valuable revenue earner, even on charter flights, filling available space not taken up by baggage. The palletised cargo is lifted out on to the roller trolleys for delivery to the cargo centre at Gatwick.

OPPOSITE PAGE, TOP RIGHT: Before the next load of passengers board, the aircraft cabin needs preparing. The aircraft cleaners board through the rear door and work their way forward.

OPPOSITE PAGE, BOTTOM LEFT: As with any engine, after a flight the engineer does an oil check, and tops up the levels.

OPPOSITE PAGE, BOTTOM RIGHT: Amongst the less glamorous but vital tasks, is toilet disposal.

MAIN PICTURE: The Leisure International 767-300ER sits on the stand at Gatwick being prepared for the next departure.

ABOVE: While the toilets are being cleared, on the other side fresh water is being topped up for the next flight.

ABOVE RIGHT: The Air BP fuel pump is connected up to the fuel metering system in the leading edge of the port wing.

ABOVE LEFT: Once connected to the pump, the fuel is delivered by underwing pressure refuelling to both sets of wing integral fuel tanks. Fuel is only delivered under the port wing with a balance being maintained during the refuelling process by ensuring that the cross-feed valves are open.

ABOVE: With the fuel feed pipes connected to the aircraft fuel system, the main fuel pipe is connected to the underground fuel delivery system, and once the connection is complete, the aircraft tanks can be loaded up for the next sortie across the North Atlantic.

MAIN PICTURE: Leisure International 767-39 HER G-UKLI is positioned by the tug ready for departure from London Gatwick in July 1998. By the start of the 1999 season, this aircraft will be in the colours of the new owners, Air 2000.

LEFT: Preparations are in hand for the next departure and the catering trolleys are ready for loading in the galleys.

ABOVE LEFT: As with all modern jet airliners, the wing is an integral fuel tank with all skin joints sealed to ensure there are no leaks.

ABOVE RIGHT: With the aircraft prepared and the crew on board, the passengers embark, some up the rear steps.

OPPOSITE PAGE, ABOVE LEFT: With the crew and passengers on board and settling in, the loading ramps are removed, soon to be followed by the last set of steps as the tug prepares for link-up.

OPPOSITE PAGE, ABOVE RIGHT: G-UKLI begins push-back ready for the next transatlantic flight.

## THE 767-400ER

The current work on the existing passenger 767 variants is to continue to refine and simplify the production, which now consist of the -200ER and -300/-300ER, the original -200 having been deleted. Safety considerations are also being progressed with the fitting of ground proximity warning systems and the reactive windsheer is being replaced by a predicted windsheer system. With the 767 fleet becoming older, product enhancements are being introduced to extend the fatigue life.

However, the major development is the 767-400, the studies for which were revealed by Boeing for the first time in April 1993 as the 767ERY. Boeing needed to consider a new long range version of the 767 in the 7,000nm (13,000km) range in competition with the Airbus A340. The new 767 development was expected to achieve 7,181nm (13,300km), compared with the existing 6,048nm (11,200km), while carrying 210 passengers in a three-class cabin layout. With the experience already gained from extended range twin-jet operations with the earlier 767-200ER and -300ER, Boeing could see that by exploiting this and looking at ways of further extending the range, was a way of keeping the type attractive. An earlier 767ERX study had provided an extra range, but had failed to generate any

interest when it was offered to the airlines in 1992. The 767ERX had involved fairly modest improvements, mainly by installing additional fuel in the horizontal stabiliser. The 767ERY doubled the additional range, but also featured a more significant modification programme. The principal focus for the changes was the wing, with the overall area and fuel capacity increased by a chord extension and increase in span. This would require an extension and strengthen of the wing box with a modified front spar. The extended wingtip would also have a winglet added. To accommodate the higher weights, the

BELOW: The next major development of the 767 is a second fuselage stretch to become the 767-400ER, the first jet airliner that has been stretched twice. In addition to the simple fuselage extension, the wing also has new 8ft (2.4m) raked wingtips, which according to wind tunnel results will give improved take-off performance and economy with less drag. The high speed model is seen inside the Boeing Transonic Wind Tunnel at Seattle. Low speed analysis has been completed in the DERA wind tunnel facility at Farnborough. *Boeing*

OPPOSITE: The Boeing 767-400ER is 21ft (6.4m) longer than the 767-300, and wherever possible is designed as a minimum change aircraft. However, the raked wingtips reduce drag, and because of the possibility of a tail scrape on take-off or landing, the undercarriage is taller. The flightdeck instrumentation can be configured by a software change to match either a 767 or 777 fleet to reduce crew training. *Boeing*

fuselage would be strengthened at section 48 over the cabin centre-section, and a strengthened undercarriage would be fitted. Additional structural modifications would be made to the rear pressure bulkhead and tail assembly.

To power this heavier model, turbofans developing 62,500lb (278kN) would be required. These improvements would give greater payload and increased range, and the more powerful engines would increase the hot and high performance. Some operators were requesting higher cruise speeds to obtain preferred routings, the increase from the existing cruise being from Mach 0.8 to between 0.82 and 0.84. Pratt & Whitney offered a new version of the PW4000 with a 4 percent improvement in fuel burn for a number of applications, including the 767 developments. The new development was expected to develop between 62,000lb and 63,000lb (275 and 280kN) of thrust, compared with the existing 60,000lb (267kN) which would put the engine in the right power capability for the 767ERY. Meanwhile GE were looking at CF-6 studies, designated the CF6-80CX with a power range of between 62,000lb (276kN) and 67,000lb (298kN).

Following a range of detailed internal studies, and discussions with the airlines to determine the needs, Boeing formerly announced what had become the 767-400ERX on 6 January 1997, the plan being to follow with a formal launch soon after, leading to a maiden flight in 1999 and certification and first deliveries the following year. The airline interest had been in an aircraft with the same range as the -300ER, but with an increased capacity. The new derivative will be capable of operating all the US domestic services as well as flying the transatlantic routes from Atlanta–London, New York–Rome and Chicago–Frankfurt. The fuselage extension of 21ft (6.4m) will be achieved by inserting two plugs either side of the centre section, increasing the two class seating capacity from 269 in the -300ER, to 303 in the -400. Maximum take-off weight will be increased to 440,924lb (200,000kg), from 412,264lb (187,000kg) of the -300ER.

Improvements to the wing aerodynamics, including canted winglets and increased span by 7m will offset the weight increase and enable the -400ERX to be flown on the same routes as the -300ER without additional fuel. It would also be possible to use the same 62,000lb (276kN) thrust P&W, GE and R-R engines making the new model very cost effective. Other design changes included an additional wing leading edge slat section outboard; a taller landing gear using 777 wheels

ABOVE: Although Boeing intended the cabin to be generally similar to the earlier models of the 767, customer demand has dictated an update on the lines of the more flexible 777. *Boeing*

and brakes to maintain adequate ground clearance during take-off rotation; increased electrical power generation from 90kVA, to 120kVA to cope with the increased demands of the in flight entertainment system; and a new APU from Allied Signal.

The 767-400ERX is designed to replace the ageing Tristars and DC-10s, as well as the older Airbus A300 and A310s. Potential airlines were looking for an easy transition from the 767-300ER, and Boeing needed one significant initial order to launch the programme, a potential requirement for 40 aircraft by Delta being the most likely one to materialise. Initially the plan was to base the cabin on the one in the 767-300, and not have the changes in concept of the 777 cabin, which would add cost and weight, and were not believed to be required by the operators. The increased capacity will require the existing air conditioning system to be modified.

There were no plans to cease production of the 767-300, unless the market demand drops, and there were also studies on fitting the new wing to the -300 fuselage to give a longer range version capable of flying between Europe and South East Asia. The development programme was expected to take up to 34 months with a May 2000 planned service entry date, requiring a formal go ahead during the third quarter of 1997. The main assembly of the new version was planned at Everett

alongside the existing 767 versions, although the Douglas Aircraft Division at Long Beach could provide additional production capacity at a later stage. All the existing partners and sub-contractors would continue to supply the production line. Rolls-Royce were thought unlikely to offer the RB211-524H as the power could not be increased to the required 62,000lb (276kN) without major technical changes.

In March 1997 Delta Air Lines and Boeing came to a controversial agreement for an deal covering a 20 year exclusive fleet renewal programme for the purchase of up to 644 aircraft. The order included the launch of the 767-400 with a firm requirement for 21 aircraft with deliveries scheduled between 2000 and 2001, as a replacement for the airline's ageing Tristar fleet, with options on a further 24 aircraft. An additional 10 767-300ERs were also ordered for delivery between 1998 and 1999, plus options on another 10 aircraft. Continental became the second customer for the 767-400 when a further long-term sole-supplier deal was announced in June 1997 including 30 767-400ERs, together with five 777-200s and an undefined number of options.

Having achieved two major orders for the 767-400, Boeing had sufficient confidence to give the full go-ahead and commence detail engineering. The CATIA design system developed for the 777 is being used extensively, and amongst other changes was the enlarging of the underfloor cargo doors. Consideration was given to the installation of a new cockpit to be compatible with the 777 and the new generation 737, which could result in an update of the existing version of the 747, 767 and the 757, especially as the latter was also being developed into a stretched version. The avionics equipment has been based on six Honeywell or Rockwell-Collins flat screen liquid crystal display (LCD) primary flight displays. This allowed software changes to make them compatible with either a mixed fleet of older 767/757s or the new 777, to reduce the cost of crew training. To achieve this, the digital displays will be programmable to display data in either a traditional round dial format or primary flight display (PFD) format.

By January 1998, Boeing had decided to incorporate the new flightdeck based on the 777, and also had decided to base the new cabin interior on the later type. Wing span had been set at 170.5ft (52m), the additional section being achieved by a composite raked tip extension with virtually twice the sweep angle, and in plane with the wing. The new main undercarriage units are 17.3in (44cm) taller and will be made from new larger forgings. To enable it to fit into the same cavity, the main gear and trunnion fittings are being moved outboard to give sufficient clearance. The fuselage extension of 21ft (6.4m) over the -300 will provide accommodation for up to 245 passengers in three classes, and 304 in a two-class configuration. The new interior was driven by the needs of the launch customers and will feature the open architecture of the 777 cabin with sculptured side wall and ceiling panels. To date two main GE engines have been offered, the CF6-80C2B7F and a more powerful -B8F version. Roll out of the first 767-400 is on schedule for August 1999.

Boeing are also studying increasing the range of the 767-400ER further to meet the requirements of potential future customers. The standard version ordered by Delta and Continental will have a base line range of 5,729nm (10,610km). However, by fitting three additional fuel tanks with a capacity of 1,448gal (6,585 litres) in the belly of the aircraft the range could be increased by a further 350nm (650km). The extra tanks could be installed behind the wingbox provisionally reserved for LD2 containers. With 241 seats, the -400 will be able to carry up to five freight pallets in the forward hold, with 18 LD2 luggage containers in the rear underfloor hold. The German charter operator Condor had shown interest in the increased capacity version, but still required the range of the -300ER. The proposed extended range version would still have the same maximum take-off weight of 450,404lb (204,300kg) of the standard -400, and Rolls-Royce had joined GE in offering an engine with their Trent 600.

## BOEING 767 FREIGHTER

In addition to its success as a passenger airliner, Boeing had been studying a specialist cargo version, to provide an intermediate capacity between the cargo versions of the 757 and the 747.

In January 1993 the long-awaited freighter version, based on the 767-300ER was launched following an initial order from United Parcel Service (UPS) for 30 aircraft, with options on a further 30. The stiff competition had been from McDonnell Douglas with the MD-11C and Airbus with the A300-600C. UPS required the 767 freighter to provide additional capacity as well as meeting the future domestic and international requirements for the medium to long range heavy lift aircraft. The 767s were also expected to replace the earlier models of the fleet of 49 DC-8s. The selection process was helped by the fleet commonality with the early 757PF, which was launched by UPS in 1987, the fleet having grown to 30 aircraft. Key factors

BELOW: The Boeing 767-300 airframe was adapted to the freighter configuration with an upward opening door on the port side of the forward cabin. This would allow all types of freight to be carried, including palletised loads and individual items, in addition to the normal underfloor cargo space. *Boeing*

included flexible payload and range capabilities. The contract announcement allowed detailed design engineering to commence, with a target completion during the second quarter of 1994 when production commenced at Everett. The flight development programme was scheduled to commence in the second quarter of 1995, with certification and delivery of the first aircraft to UPS in October.

To adapt the basic 767-300 airframe to the freighter role, Boeing added local structural strengthening to the main undercarriage, and internal wing structure, but without increasing the wing-skin thickness. The main deck floor structure was strengthened to take a load of up to 24 cargo containers and the most obvious external change is the fitting of 8.8ft (2.67m) by 11ft (3.4m) upward opening freight door on the forward port side of the fuselage. Since the batch of freighters was of a reasonable size the lack of windows was achieved within the production process, allowing the stringers to be deleted along the normal window position saving weight. Most cargo aircraft

have the windows plugged during conversion, either from an existing airframe or in new production. The 767-300 freighter can accommodate 10,065cu ft (285cu m) of cargo on the main deck, with a further 3,143cu ft (89cu m) in the lower hold. The initial target maximum take-off weight was 408,516lb (185,300kg), with a projected growth to 424,389lb (192,500kg). Maximum revenue payload varies from 101,413lb (46,000kg) over a 4,000nm (7,400km) range to 125,663lb (57,000kg) over 2,997nm (5,550km).

The battle for the engine supplier then commenced, with Rolls-Royce not only trying to gain a second customer in a P&W and GE dominated market, but also had gained an edge over P&W, when the RB211-535E4 was selected for the earlier 757PFs. In the event it was the GE CF6-80C2 engines which were selected in mid-1993 to power the 767-300 freighters. UPS therefore had the products of all three major engine suppliers on their 757/767 fleet. The decision in favour of the GE engine was the ability to deliver a new low-emission version in

time for delivery of the first freighter, a deadline which Pratt & Whitney and Rolls-Royce could not meet. Under the terms of the agreement GE modified the 62,100lb (275kN) thrust CF6-80C2B7F to reduce hydrocarbon, carbon monoxide and oxide of nitrogen emissions by some 40 per cent over the current versions of the engine. The total contract, worth about $600 million, covered 68 new engines and the spares package between 1995 and 2002 for the 30 aircraft on firm order. The options with GE covered an additional 69 engines and spares for the 30 option aircraft, with deliveries planned from 1999 to 2008. The engine/airframe combination was to be certificated with full EROPS capability.

ABOVE: Asiana ordered the first full specification Boeing 767-300F Freighter. Boeing 767-38EFER HL7507 is the first of two of this version to be delivered to the airline and is seen taking off from Everett. *Boeing/Asiana*

ABOVE LEFT: The Boeing 767 Freighter was launched by an order for 30 aircraft from UPS in January 1993. The UPS aircraft are built to a more simple specification with no cargo handling system, basic galley and toilet facilities and no fire suppression system as live cargo would not be carried. UPS 767-34AF N303UP was the third delivered to the operator, and is seen at King County Airport, the commercial side of Boeing Field at Seattle in May 1998. *Philip Birtles*

BELOW LEFT: The first 767 Freighter N301UP was handed over to UPS at Everett on 12 October 1995. It is seen here compared with a Cargolux Boeing 747-400 Freighter. *Boeing*

By September 1993 the preliminary design review (PDR) was completed, agreeing and establishing design concepts, which allowed work to commence on the engineering mock-up for completion in January 1994. The final stage of the review had taken eleven days to go through the aircraft in detail, and unusually the UPS representatives were present throughout to give their advice. It was expected that this would probably be the last mock-up built by Boeing, as although all the new design was done digitally on CATIA, it was not practical to digitalise all the previous drawings.

The freighter programme was very short, with only 31 months from go-ahead to delivery, and the mock-up allowed the Boeing engineers to evaluate the design differences of the generic 767 freighter, as the UPS version was significantly different in configuration. Amongst the differences with the UPS specification was the lack of a main-deck powered cargo handling system, no fire suppression systems for live or perishable loads, and the galley and toilet systems would be enhanced in the non-UPS aircraft. Not only was the programme tight on time for development, but following the first delivery in October 1995, UPS required a further five aircraft in time for the Christmas rush.

Boeing established the specification of the full capability generic version of the 767-300 freighter in October 1993, and the first operator to show positive interest was the South Korean airline Asiana who had a requirement for two aircraft, the first of which was delivered in mid-1996, followed by the second in 1998, fitting in with the UPS delivery programme.

Construction of the first freighter for UPS began in January 1995 with the fabrication of the front wing spar and the cargo floor loaded into the production jig. By this time over 90 per cent of the design engineering of the new variant had been released, and to ensure that there was no interruption of the passenger versions, the tool designers, planners and engineers for the freighter were on site during the assembly process,

which was later developed in the assembly of the all new 777. The first nose section of the freighter was produced at Wichita, with major fuselage assemblies being built in Japan by Mitsubishi Heavy Industries and Kawasaki Heavy Industries for delivery to Everett in January and February. The final joining of all the major sub-assemblies was achieved in mid-April and the first completed freighter was rolled out in May ready for the maiden flight of 2hr 29min in late June. The total development programme was expected to include 60 flying hours and a further 300 ground test hours. Three aircraft were used in the test programme which was short due to the need to only certificate freighter modifications. The flight testing focused on the environmental conditions, particularly the smoke detection, the smoke seal between the cockpit and the cargo compartment, and the balance of the air conditioning system. Following a successful completion of the development programme, the first 767-300 Freighter was delivered to UPS on 12 October 1995, ready to start a series of proving flights which commenced from the UPS base at Louisville, Kentucky on 16 October with a completion by the end of the month.

With the entry into service of the freighter with UPS, the US FAA gave tentative approval for instant 180-minute EROPS to the airline, but before granting full approval,

1999, and two in 2000. The 767 freighter conversions offered reliability, operating efficiency, manufacturers support, availability, and complied with environmental issues. The converted freighters are capable of carrying 74,957lb (34,000kg), and met the demand for the additional cargo capacity and served markets outgrowing the existing DC-8 freighters. The initial batch of 10 767-200s came from All Nippon Airways, the conversion being undertaken by TIMCO at Greenboro, North Carolina. The 767 conversion included cabin floor strengthening, a 9g cargo barrier net at the front of the cabin, flightdeck modifications and a new environmental control system. The other major modification was the installation of the upward opening cargo door in the forward cabin.

reviewed the UPS maintenance, operations and support systems to ensure safe EROPS operation with the 767. The EROPS qualification of the 767-300ER and the documentation and certification testing by Boeing and UPS were already largely completed, and the GE powered passenger versions of the 767-300ER had already been awarded 180-minute EROPs in 1989. An additional condition was that the 767 operations would be limited initially to USA only, while UPS and the pilots had discussions over crewing arrangements for flights longer than eight hours. For flights of this duration, the FAA require a relief crew member to be on board — either a captain or first officer, but there appeared to be disagreement on the relevant pay scale for the third crew member.

The first full specification 767-300 General Market Freighter was delivered to Asiana in August 1996. Meanwhile, Boeing were predicting a need for 600 new freighters worth $65 billion in 1995 dollars from mid-1996 to 2015, with a further 1,450 conversions from existing retired passenger airframes. As a result the US cargo carrier, Airborne Express decided to acquire 12 767-200s for conversion to freighters, with the possibility of adding another 10 to 15 over eight years, worth a total investment of $600 million. The first two conversions were planned enter service in 1997, with four each in 1998 and

## MILITARY 767S

The major military development of the 767 was an airborne warning and control system (AWACS) based on the 767-200 airframe. The previous AWACS aircraft for the USAF, NATO, RAF, France and Saudi Arabia had been based on the rather out-dated Boeing 707 airframe, which by the late 1980s was out of production. To restart the 707 production line, an order for at least 14 aircraft would have been necessary, but the 767 airframe provided a much more up to date and cost effective solution for the market for this role in the future. Boeing first revealed the 767 AWACS concept in January 1992, with the rotating radome mounted on pylons over the top of the rear cabin similar to the installation on the 707/E-3 version. The Japanese showed the most interest, as they had a need for four of these aircraft, with Australia requiring a similar number.

However, it was not a one horse race, as competition came from the Lockheed P-3 Orion AEW variant, and two versions of the C-130 Hercules. These Hercules based variants were the

General Dynamics developed C-130 AEW-C and the jointly developed Lockheed/Grumman C-130 AEW. The Japan Defence Agency (JDA) sent an evaluation team to the USA in May 1992 to evaluate the four candidates for the Japan Air Self-Defence Force AWACS requirement, the main parameters being cost, performance and development times. The Boeing candidate was the only fan jet powered contender, and also had the most up to date airframe and basic systems.

By mid-1992, the Boeing Defense and Space Group had allocated four 767-200ER airframes for potential development into an AWACS version, and following wind tunnel testing the final position for the radome housing the Westinghouse radar was fixed on section 46 of the 767 fuselage. The development team had grown to 100 personnel and was working to a tight schedule, although Japan had indicated that the purchase decision may be delayed until 1995. Other requirements were also possible from Italy, Saudi Arabia and South Korea.

The initial phase of the Boeing development plan was an approximate cost estimate to the US Government, with an evaluation of the basic structural modifications to the commercial airframe. This was the basis of the initial presentation to Japan, as part of a defence review in February 1992. The second phase, during the third quarter of 1992, took a closer look at the cost of the structural modifications, as well as changes to increase power of the engines. Because of the additional specialist equipment, additional electrical power was required including fitting a dual gearbox and generators. To provide the additional electrical power, two 150kVA generators were added to each engine bringing the total to 600kVA for the aircraft. The AWACS would therefore have sufficient electrical power to remain on station with one engine shut down, or two generators failed, the mission equipment and the start up of the APU to bring on extra power, requiring only 450kVA. Engines on offer were the GE CF6-80C2 and the P&W PW4048, with Rolls-Royce apparently not bidding. There were also concerns regarding continued supply of the specialist mission vendor equipment, as when transferring to new platforms vendors sometimes tend to cease supply, particularly for small batches which may already be out dated.

The final phase of the development plan was the contract phase, when the requirements of the customer were worked out and the detailed specification could be established. It was estimated that it would take five years from contract signature to deliver the first mission ready integrated system. The Boeing Commercial Aircraft Division had provisionally committed the first airframe for completion at the end of 1994. The 767-200ER airframe was selected because it had a 20 percent greater range than the earlier 707-320 due to the greater fuel capacity and improved fuel efficiency, giving a 10-20 percent range advantage over the E-3. During the wind tunnel testing, which consisted of 260 hours up to mid-1992, 140 hours had been in the transonic tunnel, with the balance in a low-speed tunnel. The only aerodynamic modification required was the addition of ventral fins below the tail for extra yaw stability, although they were not fitted in production.

The Westinghouse radar retained its previous configuration, the only changes required being the routing of the wave guide from the Klystron power amplifiers to the antenna. The 767 fuel tanks were modified to incorporate ethylene glycol-water heat exchangers for cooling the radar system. Other equipment changes from the E-3 include replacing the ARC-165 HF radio with a more modern unit and fitting the antenna in the vertical fin. Have Quick A-NETS UHF were fitted, similar to those used on the RAF E-3s, and the 767 also houses a class II Joint Tactical Distribution System terminal in the tail cone. For greater endurance, a flight refuelling receptacle was provided for 15.7in (0.4m) off the centreline, above and aft of the forward door on the port side. This gave a potential extended on station time of up to 24 hours.

BELOW: The major military development of the Boeing 767 airframe is the E-767 AWACS aircraft. The programme was launched by an order for two aircraft from the Japanese government in November 1993, followed later by an order for two more E-767s. First flight with the rotadome installed was in August 1996 with delivery of the first two aircraft in March 1998. *Boeing*

Following the completion as a basic airframe at Everett, the aircraft was flown to Wichita for conversion. This conversion involved replacing eight fuselage frames and nine floor beams in section 46 with strengthened structures to support the radome. Wichita were also responsible for the installation of a large Sundstrand produced electrical power and generation system. The modified aircraft were then flown to Everett and later Boeing Field at Seattle for the installation of the specialist mission equipment and radar, and the full integration with flight testing.

With a large number of ageing military derivatives of the 707 still in service with the USAF, Boeing were naturally keen to offer an effective replacement. As well as promoting the AWACS concept, Boeing were keen for the USAF to switch from 707 airframes to new 767s for the joint-surveillance-target-attack radar system (JSTARS) being developed by Grumman. In greater numbers are the KC-135 tanker and transport versions, the 767 tanker/transport being capable of being fitted with a flying boom and probe and drogue systems used respectively by the USAF and the US Navy. The 767 VC-X was proposed as a replacement for the VC-137 VIP transports operated by the 89th Military Airlift Wing at Andrews Air Force Base. This unit is responsible for all government VIP transport and had three VC-137Bs which were due for retirement in 1993, and four VC-137Cs, of which two had formerly served as Air Force One aircraft for Presidential use. Despite being in excellent condition, there were seen to be problems with supporting such old aircraft and their equipment.

With some 600 KC-135 tanker/transports remaining in service well into the next century, many having been re-engined with more efficient fan engines, there was no immediate urgency for their replacement, but it would not be possible to replace them all at once, and therefore a phased programme was suggested. The support of the AWACS was also expected to include a requirement for tanker support, and the similar airframe would reduce logistical and support problems.

In mid-1993 Turkey expressed an interest in the E-767, as the programme had become known, and Boeing began the process of gaining the US Congressional approval before proceeding with the negotiations. Meanwhile, the Japanese Government had confirmed their intention to buy four of the E-767 systems, with a contract for the first two aircraft in negotiation for signature later in the year for delivery in 1998, and the follow on contract expected to be signed in 1994. All the Japanese aircraft were to be equipped with nine two crew standard mission consoles, and without an air-to-air refuelling capability.

The long anticipated launch order for the E-767 AWACS was finally received in November 1993 from Japan. The Boeing Defence and Space Group was awarded a foreign military sales contract for two aircraft, by the USAF Electronics Centre at Hanscom AFB, Massachusetts. This part of the order worth $408 million covered the integration and installation of the specialist AWACS prime mission equipment, acceptance testing and delivery of the aircraft. The balance of the contract worth $840 million was placed by Itochu of Japan, which covered the cost of the two 767 airframes and GE CF6-80C2 engines. Both the aircraft were scheduled for delivery in early 1998, and the last elements of the contract will be fulfiled by October 1999.

In early 1995 Boeing formally announced the intention to develop a combined military tanker/transport version of the 767, the JASDF being the primary target customer, with other prospects being a military tanker/freighter for Saudi Arabia and possibly South Korea. In the long term Boeing continued to promote the 767 as a replacement for the USAF KC-135 tanker transports, although the Boeing 757 was selected for the VC-137 replacement as the C-32A in August 1996.

Boeing were offering two versions of the tanker/transport Multi-Mission aircraft based on the 767-200ER and the longer 767-300ER. Each version would feature a rear underfuselage mounted refuelling boom as well as two underwing pods for the probe and drogue refuelling system. The boom operation was to be from the cabin with the assistance of a rearward facing camera. The larger -300ER tanker/transport would be able to accommodate up to seven additional underfloor fuel tanks, each with a capacity of 990gal (4,500 litres), and it would be capable of transferring more than 154,323lb (70,000kg) of fuel up to a range of 500nm (925km). For the transport role, the aircraft would incorporate the modifications already developed for the freighter with the side cargo door and reinforced main deck. This would allow the aircraft to carry 168 passengers, or 16 pallets capable of containing up to 74,957lb (34,000kg) of cargo over ranges of up to 4,995nm (9,250km).

The JASDF was understood to have an initial requirement for six to eight tankers to support what had now become a fleet

of four E-767s, although they only had provision for a refuelling receptacle, as well as the McDonnell Douglas F-15s. The first pair of E-767s were due for hand over in March 1998, with the other pair to follow in January 1999. The requirement was expected to increase to 14 tankers, sufficient to cover Japan's north, south and western air defence regions and the JASDF were hoping to add between four and eight more E-767s to their fleet. Boeing planned to deliver the first 767 tanker/transport 40 months after the programme launch which would be defined by the number of aircraft and the quality of the customer. Although the Japanese Defence Agency (JDA) were expected to approve funding in the fiscal year of 1997, this decision is still awaited in mid-1998.

The initial E-767 airframe was ferried from Everett to Wichita in mid-October 1994 for the extensive conversion work to be carried out, before returning to Everett in June 1996. This first E-767 for the JASDF commenced the flight development programme from Everett on 9 August 1996 complete with the AWACS radome fitted. The initial flight of 2hr 55min was the start of a seven-month test programme before the installation of the prime mission equipment. The early part of the test programme consisted of flight and handling qualities under US FAA rules for a supplemental type certificate under Part 25. By certificating to commercial standards, Boeing believed that this would give an export advantage. It would give an aircraft clear of any US Government and USAF involvement, leaving the latitude to satisfy offset requirements.

The second aircraft was delivered from Everett to Wichita at the end of 1996 to be fitted with the complete suite of mission equipment for systems qualification testing. The two test aircraft then operated in parallel to achieve certification in early 1998. The flight testing included checking flutter clearances, buffet boundaries and fuel consumption performance. The endurance at 1,000nm (1,850km) from base was expected to be up to seven hours. One of the main priorities of the test effort was to check the operation of the modified electrical power distribution and generation system. To provide sufficient power for the aircraft systems, each of the 767's CF6-80C2 engines

were fitted with two 150kVA generators in place of the standard 90kVA units. The APU also supports a fifth 90kVA generator, giving a total potential output of 690kVA.

Flight testing of the first aircraft went so well that the programme was completed three weeks ahead of schedule, after flying 383 hours in 130 flights. The aircraft then underwent an instrument refurbishment at Boeing Field, before returning to Wichita for the flight test equipment to be removed. It then returned to Seattle in May for the installation and integration of the mission systems, flight testing of the second aircraft beginning the following month. Once completed, the first two E-767s were handed over to the Japanese Government at Boeing Field on 11 March 1998, with the second pair of E-767s alongside being prepared for their completion in early 1999.

Meanwhile towards the end of 1996, Israel Aircraft Industries (IAI) offered to South Korea the Phalcon phased array airborne early warning (AEW) radar system integrated into a Boeing 767. The Elta system being proposed was based on the multi sensor L-band Phalcon package already in operation in a 707 with the Chilean Air Force. The 767 configuration would feature an additional rear fuselage mounted antenna to give the full 360 degree coverage. It was anticipated that the aft antenna would provide 100 degrees of coverage out to 180nm (333km). The two conformal side arrays mounted on each side of the forward fuselage scan through 80 degrees out to 244nm (425km), or when employed with the nose mounted array can scan a 260 degree sector at a range of 200nm (370km). The long range 767-300ER version was the preferred choice with a maximum unrefuelled range of 5,400nm (8,140km), an endurance of up to 10.5 hours, a speed of Mach 0.75 and an operating ceiling of 35,000ft (10,675m).

The 767 Phalcon would have the capability to deal with up to 500 targets in either track-while-scan or full track mode. The large cabin would be able to accommodate up to 11 operator stations compared with the four radar and two electronic and communications support measures (ESM and CSM) consoles fitted in the Chilean 707. The 767 would be fitted with the same IFF system and Elta EL/L-8300 0.5 to 18GHz ESM as fitted to the 707 with an optional frequency coverage of 18 to 40GHz. By making E-Systems the prime contractor for the CSM, the South Korean aircraft would have voice and datalink interoperability with the US military. South Korea were expected to issue requests for tender in early 1997 with a decision on which system to adopt in 1998, but at the time of writing no moves have been made in the selection process. The competing bids with IAI are the Boeing 767 Airborne Warning and Control System, fitted with a conventional rotodome and Westinghouse SPY-2 radar, while Saab and Ericsson proposed the Erieye phased array radar, the South Korean requirement being for four AEW aircraft.

# 5 IN SERVICE

## ETOPS/EROPS

Apart from the normal challenges of the introduction of a new airliner, the Boeing 767 had to prove itself capable of flying regularly non-stop over the oceans of the world to make full use of its range and payload capability. The particular challenge for the 767 was that it was a twin-engine aircraft that had to be capable of continuing to fly safely on one engine if the other one failed. The modern fan-jet engines have built up an unrivalled reputation for efficiency and reliability — especially when compared with the powerful commercial piston engines of the post-war period when it was not uncommon for an arrival at the destination on only three engines. Because of the unreliability of these piston engines and the early jet engines, the US Federal Airworthiness Authority (FAA) issued in 1953 FAR Part 121.161. This regulation stipulated that,

*'Unless authorised to do so by the administration on the basis of the nature of the terrain, the type of operation or the performance of the aircraft involved, no holder of a transport licence shall operate a twin-engine aircraft on a route which at any point lies more than one hour flying time, in zero wind and at normal single engine cruising speed, from an adequate airport.'*

Although this rule applies theoretically only to US registered aircraft, its influence in practice is on a much wider scale, affecting the operators of most of the US-built or operated airliners, in addition to the conditions being adopted by many other airworthiness authorities, including the British CAA.

However, with the deregulation of the US airline industry and the increased fuel costs, world airlines were looking for the most economic aircraft available. It was very costly to fly the high capacity four-engine Boeing 747 and the large Tristar and DC-10 trijets on the long thin routes with an unacceptable number of empty seats. To give an example, it cost some US$56,000 to fly a 747 from St Louis–Paris with seating for 370 passengers. On the same route a Boeing 767 could carry 190 passengers for US$30,000 giving a 46 percent reduction and maintaining the cost per passenger almost constant. However, the real saving is on fuel costs, the 747 burning 2,508gal (11,400 litres) of fuel per hour, compared with the 767 at 1,078gal (4,900 litres) per hour. If the 747 is full, then the costs are justified, but on the less popular routes there can be a very serious economic disadvantage. The 767 also makes a more modest saving in being operated by two crew, while the earlier 747s and trijets needed three crew.

ABOVE: Delta Air Lines became the second customer for the 767 when an order was placed for 15 GE CF6-80A powered aircraft in November 1978. Delta followed with orders for 14 CF-6 powered 767-300s, but when ordering the 767-300ER, the engine selected was the P&W PW.4060. Delta 767-332 N135DL is in the queue for departure at the airline base at Atlanta, Georgia in January 1993. *Philip Birtles*

LEFT: The first airline to order and put the Boeing 767 into service was United Airlines, a long term customer of Boeing. The initial order for 19 Pratt & Whitney JT9D-7R4D powered 767-200/200ERs was placed in July 1978 with first delivery in August 1982. United 767-222ER N607UA *City of Denver*, the 10th aircraft off the line, is seen at London Heathrow in June 1991. *Philip Birtles*

Boeing studies found that during the piston era in the 1950s, taking a fleet of 200 piston engine airliners, a double engine failure could be expected on average once every 16 years, let alone a single engine failure. With the advances in reliability of current generation jet engines, the likelihood of a double engine failure in a fleet of 200 767s had failed to one in every 40,000 years. Engine reliability and maintenance has increased to such an extent, that the most common reasons for shutting down one engine during flight is the failure of an associated system, crew miss-selection or spurious warnings. Efforts were therefore made to improve the reliability of the supporting systems, especially as when an engine really does fail, the remaining engine and associated systems are working that much harder.

With the economy and greater endurance of the modern twin jet airliner, the aircraft were used initially for longer routes over land, to give an opportunity to prove the reliability. However, the airliner does not know if it is flying over land or water. With the existing regulations, the 767 could fly typically no more than 400nm (741km) from a suitable diversionary air-field, but Boeing was naturally keen to expand on the use of the aircraft on longer ranges.

The TWA batch of 10 767s ordered in December 1979 were configured with the maximum possible fuel capacity, including a wing centre-section fuel tank, to allow the aircraft to be flown on long range routes. In 1983 TWA flew their first US non-stop transcontinental service, demonstrating over a period of time the required performance in terms of range and navigational accuracy. To support these results, Boeing made a non-stop flight in a 767 from Lisbon–Seattle, and soon after TWA commenced scheduled non-stop transatlantic flights from the USA to Europe, but still flying to the original 60-minute rule. Since this did not achieve the optimum economy and operational advantage, TWA requested the authority to operate to the ICAO defined advisory 90-minute rule, increasing the distance to a suitable diversionary airfield to 690nm (1,278km) on one engine.

Before the FAA would authorise these flights, five of the 767s had to be modified with the collaboration of Boeing, at the cost of US$3 million per aircraft — a considerable investment. As well as the remaining engine and associated systems having to work harder, the operating crew would have greater demands to fly the aircraft. In addition to greater reliability of the engines, systems integrity had to be enhanced. The remaining engine-driven generator or hydraulic pump could be subject to overload, the twin jet systems integrity having to be at least as

ABOVE: TWA ensured that the 767-200s they ordered in December 1979 had the maximum fuel capacity to allow unrestricted EROPS. Following additional modifications to the aircraft, the airline were able to commence transatlantic operations under the 120-minute rule on 28 April 1985. TWA 767-205ER started with TWA, but has operated in a number of other countries with the registrations LN-SUV, N767BE, PP-VNL, N90549, G-BNAX and finally back to TWA. It is seen at London Luton Airport in October 1987 after being repainted by Britannia in TWA colours. *Philip Birtles*

good overall as that of the multi-engine aircraft. For example the life expectancy of an electrical generator is significantly diminished once it starts to carry the loads alone, requiring an assessment of its likely failure rate under the more demanding conditions. In the early days the auxiliary power unit (APU) was not as reliable as they have become today, and therefore they could not be expected to start every time after a cold soak at altitude. The battery power would generally be insufficient for long periods, and the ram-air turbine (RAT) only provided

sufficient emergency electrical power to operate the basic controls. When leaving on a long range twin-engine flight, the allowable deficiencies on departure are reduced, and the diversionary airfield must have sufficient aids to permit a recovery in poor weather, as well as having an adequate length of runway.

Included amongst the modifications made by TWA and Boeing was an additional 5kVA hydraulically driven electrical generator, a higher capacity avionics cooling system, additional HF radio, a fire detection and extinguishing system in the underfloor cargo areas and extra life rafts for overwater operation. In addition, whenever the flight duration exceeded eight hours, an additional crew member was carried on the flight-deck, whether the flight was over land or water.

As an ongoing development of long-range twin-jet operations, TWA inaugurated on 28 April 1985 twin engine scheduled operations between St Louis–Paris applying the FAA 120-minute rule which gave an average distance from a diversionary

airfield of 800nm (1,482km), but additional equipment had to be fitted to comply with the more demanding conditions. It was not long before TWA were joined by American Airlines, Air Canada and El Al, all operating transatlantic services between the USA and Europe with 767s, while on the other side of the world, Qantas were operating a number of long range twin engine routes from Sydney and Melbourne.

While Boeing would like all restrictions removed, the airlines are generally happy with the 120-minute rule, as it removes all the major restrictions. In a period of five months, TWA operated 1,500 transatlantic crossings, building up to 16 a day with the 767. During that time diversions were made on only four occasions, (three times for compressor stalling, and once for a false oil contents indication). On each occasion the aircraft was able to reach its designated diversion on one engine without problem, and after inspection the aircraft was able to continue the flight without any repair being necessary.

Although TWA had pioneered regular twin-engine transatlantic operations, it was in fact El Al who inaugurated services from the North America to Europe with 767s in March 1984, when a flight was made from Montreal–Tel Aviv in 11 hours 8 minutes non-stop. During the 1985 summer season Air Canada flew more than 200 North Atlantic crossings, from Halifax–Prestwick and then to London, operating within the 60-minute rule, replacing Tristars, and not experiencing any diversions, engine shut-downs or power emergencies.

From December 1983 until the end of 1985, Air Canada had operated more than 600 twin-engine overwater flights between Canada and the Caribbean. By fitting a fourth electrical generator and extra fire protection to the 767s, Air Canada were able to fly a distance equivalent to 138 minutes from the nearest diversion airfield, the longest sector on these routes being the 2,275nm (4,213km) from Toronto–Port of Spain. The minimum departure requirements were three serviceable

ABOVE: El Al commenced EROPS from North America to Europe with 767s in March 1984, flying non-stop Montreal –Tel Aviv in 11hrs 8min. El Al ordered two P&W JT9D-7R4D powered 767-200s in March 1981, followed by a pair of 767-200ERs. El Al 767-258ER 4X-EAD was the last of the four delivered, and is seen on finals to Hong Kong Kai Tak in April 1998. *Philip Birtles*

RIGHT: During the summer of 1985, Air Canada operated more than 200 transatlantic crossings from Halifax–Prestwick using the ETOPS 60-minute rule before flying on to London and did not experience any engine related problems. Air Canada 767-233ER C-GDSS is seen on final approach to London Heathrow in May 1992. *Philip Birtles*

generators and the APU. The extended range twin-jet operations (ETOPS) systems integrity was tested by Air Canada on the initial delivery flight from Seattle–Montreal when the APU was started after a cold soak at 41,000ft (12,497m), and was used to provide power to a variety of electrical systems. The aircraft's main electrical power sources were deliberately interrupted, the ER generator powering up the essential loads, which combined with the APU, gave the desired protection.

Qantas began ETOPS operations with flights across the South Pacific and Tasman Sea, the longest leg being 3,870nm (7,167km) from Brisbane–Tokyo, with a maximum diversion time of 104 minutes. Qantas were joined on the 767ER routes across the Tasman Sea by Air New Zealand, who also flew the aircraft on additional routes. American Airlines commenced 767-200ER flights from Chicago to Geneva and Zürich on 1 April 1986, later linking Dallas/Fort Worth to Frankfurt and London, later increasing capacity with the 767-300ERs. Although ETOPS operations were not just the responsibility of the engine manufacturers, they played a key part.

Amongst the FAA requirements for ETOPS approval, was that an engine should have completed a fleet total of 250,000 hours in the air, of which 75,000 must be on the specific airframe for which the approval is requested. The GE CF6-80C2-powered 767s achieved this milestone in May 1988, gaining FAA approval for 120-minute ETOPS flights. The engine had demonstrated a very high level of reliability, with only four in-flight shut-downs — equivalent to a failure rate of 0.009 per 1,000 flying hours. Pratt & Whitney gained FAA approval in April 1990 for 120-minute ETOPS for 767s powered by the PW4000 engines, soon after achieving 180-minute ETOPS for the earlier more-proven JT9D-7R4-equipped aircraft.

In addition to the engines, and additional special equipment gaining approval for ETOPS, each individual airline also had to achieve the approval of their own airworthiness authority to undertake the long range overwater services, since their maintenance, training and flight operations had to comply with much higher standards.

By mid-1988 some 100 ETOPS-compliant 767s were in operation with 17 airlines, achieving more than 1,500 flights per month, building the vital experience and confidence in the concept. These continuing flights amounted to around 32,000 extended range flights overall, of which 52 had successfully diverted or returned to the starting point.

Having established the practicality of the 120-minute rule,

the next step was to move to the 180-minute standard, the CF6-80C2-powered 767s being the closest to achieving the requirements. However, there was some criticism that running a single engine for three hours at increased thrust to a suitable diversionary airfield might cause an overload and reduce reliability. Boeing pointed out in support of the increased ETOPS capability, that an engine is working much harder on take-off and climb out, (what with the higher temperatures and stresses) than on a long slow cruise following an engine shut down. The granting of the 180-minute rule would allow more direct southerly routes across the North Atlantic, saving fuel, and furthermore the Pacific would be opened up to extended range twin-jet operations. By 1988 some 40 percent of 767 extended range operations were transatlantic, and another 50 percent had been accumulated by Qantas and Air New Zealand across the Tasman Sea and other Asian routes.

At the beginning of 1989, American Airlines were working with the FAA to achieve approval for flights with the GE powered 767-300ERs on the Dallas–Hawaii route. This would be the first route to break the 120-minute rule, and it could only be exceeded following a programme of FAA observed validation flights resulting in the clearance being extended to 180-minutes from the nearest diversion. This would permit twin engine jet airliners to fly up to 1,200nm (2,222km) from the nearest airport — effectively giving coverage of all world-wide routes — which was of particular significance across the Pacific.

There was less priority in Europe to adopt the 180-minute rule, because the 120-minute rule covered most of the Atlantic, the need for the 180-minute rule only being on routes from Europe to Brazil and North Africa to Central America. Generally these routes required an intermediate landing for commercial reasons, and therefore did not cause a problem.

Before granting a 120-minute dispensation, the British CAA required that an engine type must have a shut down rate of less than 0.05 per 1,000 flights, with the ultimate goal of 0.03 per 1,000 flights. To progress to 180-minute qualification, better than 0.02 shut downs per 1,000 flights would need to be demonstrated. In early 1989, the term ETOPS was replaced by EROPS (Extended Range OPerationS), the reasoning behind this being that all long range airliners should have the same high reliability and safety standards, regardless of the number of engines. A particular example of this is cargo hold fire protection, suppression and containment.

In September 1989 Rolls-Royce and BA were working towards the 120-minute EROPS approval for the 767-300 fitted with the RB211-524G/H engines with a target for achievement with the CAA in 1991. At least the engines were also gaining maturity and reliability levels while powering the airline's 747s. In April 1991 the FAA approval was granted for 120-minute EROPS following no unscheduled removals or shut-downs over more than half a million flying hours.

The CAA approval for 110-minute EROPS followed in 1992 to allow BA to fly the 767s across the North Atlantic to New York for the less dense schedules.

## IN SERVICE

The launch order for the Boeing 767 came from United Airlines for 30 aircraft on 14 July 1978 after a close run competition with the Airbus A310. The 44,300lb **(000kN)**-thrust P&W JT9D-7R, derated from the engines used on the United 747s were selected after a hard fought contest with GE. Options for a further 37 767s were placed in November, the total value of the order being around $1,200 million, of which Pratt & Whitney had a $200 million share. The deliveries were scheduled to start in mid-1982, and be completed during 1984.

In early 1982, despite earlier sales successes, there became a slow down in the market caused by a number of factors. The US economy was failing to make any significant recovery from the recession which gripped it, there were air traffic control delays as the system became re-established following the dismissals by the government of the air traffic controllers the previous year and the US government were restricting landing slot allocations at 22 major American airports, interfering with the free market system.

With FAA certification of the Pratt & Whitney powered 767s being achieved on 30 July, the first 767 was handed over to Richard J Ferris, chairman and chief executive of United Airlines, by Boeing president Malcolm T. Stamper on 19 August 1982 at the Everett factory. This was the ninth 767 off the production line and was used to inaugurate commercial services from Chicago–Denver on 8 September. Four more 767s

were delivered to United by the end of October, increasing to eight aircraft by early 1983, and a further 11 aircraft by the end of May. With the growing fleet of 767s, they were able to operate services to San Francisco, New York and Boston, and from October 1982, Portland, Seattle and Detroit were added. By 1 November, United was serving 11 US destinations with the average daily utilisation up to 8.2 hours per aircraft. Despatch reliability of the total 767 fleet with all airlines reached 95.1 percent by the end of the year. The remaining 20 of the initial firm order were deferred for the time being, and rescheduled for delivery at the rate of five a year from 1985 to 1988, (instead of all deliveries being completed by the end of 1984). By the middle of 1993 United operated a fleet of 19 767-200s and 23 767-300ERs.

The first GE-powered 767 for Delta commenced its flight development programme in February 1982 flying 315 hours on engine certification. The second 767 for Delta Airlines was exhibited at the Farnborough Air Show in September 1982 contributing about 40 hours of long range flying, much of it to Farnborough and back. FAA certification of the CF6-80A powered 767 was awarded in early October, clearing the way for delivery to the launch customers of both Delta and American Airlines. During the route proving flights fuel efficiency was 6.6 percent better than predicted over a typical 1,000nm (1,852km) stage. Up to the end of 1985, Delta had been profitable for 37 out of 38 years of its existence and the

ABOVE: Air New Zealand was able to allocate the Boeing 767s to ETOPS flights across the Tasman Sea from New Zealand to Australia. Air New Zealand 767-319ER ZK-NCE, on lease from ILFC, is seen on arrival at Sydney in December 1992. *Philip Birtles*

ABOVE LEFT: Qantas used the ETOPS capability of the 767 from Australia to as far afield as Tokyo with a maximum diversion time of 104 minutes. Qantas 767-338ER VH-OGI *City of Port Agusta* is seen approaching the terminal at Sydney in December 1992. *Philip Birtles*

39,000 employees were mainly non-union and had a strong loyalty towards the company. When due to declining traffic and other economic problems, Delta made its first quarterly financial loss in mid-1982, unlike many other airlines, no staff were laid off. As a mark of their gratitude, on their own initiative the staff raised $30 million to buy a 767, partly by authorising a percentage of salary from the payroll, and also by direct contributions. The aircraft N102DA named *Spirit of Delta* was delivered together with N103DA on 25 October 1982.

Delta is one of the largest airlines in the USA, and at the time was carrying up to 37 million passengers annually to 106 domestic cities as well as to foreign destinations in Canada, Britain, Germany, France, Bermuda and the Bahamas. Delta's principal hub and main base is Atlanta from where 767 services commenced on 15 December. The fleet content was altered to include 15 767-200s, the last, N115DA being delivered on 28 February 1984, to be followed by nine 767-300 and 18 options signed for on 21 February 1984. Delta ordered six more 767-300s in May 1987 with deliveries starting the following February. Then in September 1988 as part of a major series of new orders, Delta contracted for nine 767-300ERs with options on a further 16. In mid-1991 Delta brought its total fleet of 767s to 59 aircraft with an order for another two 767-300ERs.

American Airlines received their first 767 on 4 November 1982, inaugurating services from San Francisco–New York on

21 November with the aircraft configured to carry up to 24 first class and 180 economy class passengers. By 1984 10 767-200s had been delivered with further deliveries scheduled at the rate of three in 1985 and 1986, four in 1987 and five each in 1988 and 1989. By the end of 1985 American were operating 13 767-200s and two 767-200ERs with 10 767-200s and five 767-200ERs remaining to be delivered. American Airlines also placed the launch order for the stretched 767-300ER powered by the CF6-80C2 engines to be used on their newly acquired European routes with accommodation for up to 215 passengers. Deliveries commenced in early 1988, and 11 more were ordered in mid 1991 for delivery continuing into 1998.

The first 767 deliveries outside the USA were to Air Canada on 30 October 1982 as replacement for their DC-8s which were phased out by mid-1983. However, the introduction was delayed by industrial action taken by the pilots who refused to fly the new aircraft on the route-proving programme before service introduction on 1 January 1983. The airline had offered the pilots a reduction in salary because of the perceived simpler operation of the 767, despite the savings made by dispensing with the flight engineer. By the end of January agreement had been ratified by the Canadian Airline Pilots' Association, and services commenced on 14 February serving the Toronto–Calgary, Calgary–Toronto–Montreal–San Francisco and San Francisco routes.

With Canada suffering from the economic depression resulting in poor prevailing market conditions, in July 1983 Air Canada postponed their options for six aircraft. The airline had to cut back on a number of routes, in tandem with frequency reduction on others; by this time there were four 767s in operation with two more joining the fleet by the end of the year. Anticipating an improvement in the economic situation, Air Canada felt able to order four 767-200ERs in July 1987 with options on six more, and deliveries scheduled to commence in 1988. The next year three more 767-200ERs were ordered in addition to the 15 held on option, and in September 1989 six 767-300ERs were ordered with options on nine more.

The first 767 was delivered to TWA on 22 November 1982, commencing daily scheduled services between Washington Dulles–Los Angeles and San Francisco on 9 December. Normally domestic operations are flown from the downtown Washington National Airport beside the Potomac River, but no

BELOW: American Airlines commenced flights from the USA to Europe on 1 April 1996 with 767-200ERs on ETOPS operations. American 767-223ER N332AA is seen on push-back at Manchester Airport in October 1987, ready for departure back to the USA. *Philip Birtles*

wide bodied jet airliners are permitted to operate from this airport. By mid-1986 TWA had six 767s in operation. The first of four 767s were delivered to Pacific Western on 4 March 1983, followed by the second aircraft in June. However, the order book took another modest reduction, when Pacific Western substituted four 737s for one of the remaining 767s on order.

The first operator in Asia, and indeed outside North America, was China Airlines who took delivery of their first 767 on 20 December 1982 commencing services on 1 January 1983 on the Taipei–Hong Kong–Bangkok routes, with special permission to overfly Vietnam, and soon achieved load factors of over 90 percent.

In the spring of 1983 the battle for sales between Airbus and Boeing was continuing in the international market particularly in the Middle East and Africa, and an example is that in

recent years although China Airlines operate Boeing 747-400s, the 767s have been replaced by A300-600s which are now seen regularly at Hong Kong. Ansett of Australia delayed their deliveries by six months from November 1982, until the first 767 arrived on 7 June 1983, with three more delivered by August.

Meanwhile the maximum take off weight of the 767 was increased by 15,000lb (6,804kg) to 315,000lb (142,881kg) allowing a 2,000lb (907kg) increase in payload or an increase in range of 760 statute miles (1,223km). This improvement was achieved by FAA approved changes to the flight manuals, and could be applied to the entire fleet, China Airlines being the first to take advantage of this improvement.

The first 767 commercial operation in Europe was by El Al who not liking to miss the opportunity of earning some rev-

TOP: As American Airlines built up experience with extended range twin engined operations across the Pacific from Dallas to Hawaii, breaking the 120-minute rule for the first time using GE powered 767-300ERs. On the other side of the world, American 767-323ER N360AA is seen on final approach to London Heathrow in April 1992. *Philip Birtles*

ABOVE: Ordered in June 1997, BA 767-336ER G-BZHB was delivered a year later as the second 767 to feature the new livery. It is seen on approach to London Heathrow in August 1998. *Philip Birtles*

RIGHT: Air Europe Italy operated 767-3YOER EI-CLR in the 1995 season and it is seen on turnaround at Rhodes in September. It had previously carried the registrations PT-TAF and XA-SKY. *Philip Birtles*

enue, used their first of four aircraft on its delivery flight on 12 July 1983 by carrying 100 passengers from Heathrow–Tel Aviv. Regular twice a week services were started (with the first in November) between the two destinations; El Al also replaced Boeing 707s on some African and European destinations.

The El Al aircraft could carry up to 206 tourist and 18 business class passengers and the second 767 was delivered in September. The third and fourth aircraft were 767-200ERs delivered in 1984 for transatlantic operations, El Al being the

first operator of the extended range version when it was delivered in April, later putting the aircraft on the Tel Aviv–Montreal service.

With the order by Qantas for six 767-200ERs in September 1983, the sales famine appeared to be broken, the firm order book then reaching 180 aircraft. Qantas selected the Pratt & Whitney engines and the cabins were configured for 18 business class and up to 196 economy class passengers. Qantas stated that the 767 provided the most economic means of transporting tourists around Australia, serving such destinations as Adelaide, Cairns, Darwin and Townsville. The first two 767s were planned to enter service in October 1985, with the balance of four arriving by March 1986.

The first aircraft, VH-EAJ *City of Woolongong*, was delivered some three months early on 3 July 1985, and the initial order was completed with VH-EAO *City of Cairns* on 31 March 1986. Commercial services commenced on 30 July from Melbourne–Wellington, and as the fleet grew, Wellington was also linked with Sydney and Brisbane. As further aircraft were delivered services were added to Christchurch and Auckland, followed by flights to Singapore from Adelaide, Townsville and Darwin. The route expansion continued to Noumea, and as an extension of the New Guinea operations, flights continued on to Manila. From 1 April 1986 new 767 routes included Perth–Tokyo and Brisbane–Cairns–Tokyo, the passenger loads being supplemented by perishable cargoes such as fresh meat, fruit, vegetables and seafood on all the international flights.

In May 1987, Qantas ordered their first 767-300ER with options on a further six and selected the 60,800lb (267kN) thrust GE CF6-80C2 engines because they had been cleared for extended range operations over water, which the P&W engines were still to achieve. Qantas confirmed two of the options on the 767-300ERs in November 1987, for delivery by March 1989, converting another option in April 1988 and a

further one in July for delivery by the end of 1989. Another four 767-300ERs were ordered in early 1990 expanding the routes throughout Asia.

A unique feature of five of the early Qantas 767-200s was that, due to union pressure, they were configured with a three crew flight deck to include a flight engineer. However, in September 1995 the decision was made to reconfigure these aircraft to two crew configuration to give commonality across the fleet and save some US$2.6 million annually.

On 29 September 1983 Japan Airlines placed a significant order for 767s to replace their DC-8s. The total order was for nine aircraft with six options, the firm orders consisting of four 767-200s, two 767-200ERs and the launch order for three of the stretched 767-300s, the total value being $560 million. The delivery schedule called for three -200s in 1986, one in 1987 and the two 767ERs in 1988. The delivery of the 767-300s commenced in 1987 with plans for two per year from 1988 until 1991, bringing the total to15 aircraft. The 767s are used on the thinner routes around the Asian region mixing the -200s and -300s according to the anticipated capacity requirements.

In November 1983 there were strong rumours circulating that Kuwait Airways were considering three 767-200ERs, but the interest was not confirmed by Boeing. This was a tantalising prospect, as the airline was already an operator of Airbus A300-600 and A310s, the mix of the two different products appearing not to be justified for operational and support reasons, since either of the manufacturers products could satisfy the route requirements. However, in September 1984 Kuwait Airways confirmed their order for the three 767-200ERs and used three yet to be delivered A310s in part exchange.

Although the two types have a similar passenger capacity, it was claimed that the 767 had a longer range, greater cargo capacity and was more fuel efficient. The first Pratt & Whitney powered 767 was delivered on 20 March 1986, to be operated alongside the existing Airbus fleet. On what was claimed to be the longest flight by a twin-jet airliner up to that time, was the delivery of a subsequent 767 from Seattle–Kuwait on 20 July 1986. The 7,893 statute mile (12,703km) flight was completed in a time of 14 hours 12 minutes. With the rapid and unexpected start of the Gulf War, Kuwait Airways was only able to save one of their 767s from the invading forces, the other two being flown to Baghdad, where they were eventually wrecked during the Allied air attacks.

Another Middle Eastern order came from Egyptair, who signed a contract for three P&W JT9D-7R4E powered 767-200ERs in January 1984, with deliveries starting in July. The Egyptair aircraft had the fuel capacity increased from 16,700 US gal (63,209 litres) to 20,000 US gal (75,700 litres) by utilising part of the centre-section tank capacity, allowing the full payload of 206 passengers in a three class layout with their baggage and additional cargo to be carried up to 5,700 miles (9,173km). With the arrival of the new aircraft, they began replacing 707s on the Middle Eastern regional routes, as well as European and African services. In June 1988 Egyptair ordered two of the stretched 767-300ERs, and in October a further two 767-200ERs were also ordered.

Britannia Airways had been a loyal Boeing customer for many years with a large fleet of 737-200s. With a need for greater capacity over longer ranges, the airline placed an initial order for three 767-200s, the first of which, G-BKVZ was delivered to Luton Airport on 8 February 1984. Configured for inclusive tour operations, the cabin could carry up to 273   passengers and amongst a number of innovations at the time were central toilets, large overhead bins, custom built galleys to supply the larger load of passengers and video systems to provide safety information.

The first Britannia 767 commercial operation was on 18 February from Luton to Tunisia, with Manchester added to the departures the following week. The second 767 followed by the end of the month, with the third delivered in spring 1985, a fourth having been ordered in May 1984. With a range of 2,800nm (5,186km), the 767s were initially used on the more popular European destinations from Luton, Manchester and Gatwick, including Palma, Alicante, Malaga, Tenerife, Athens and Corfu, but had the capability of serving more distant destinations in Australia, West Africa, the Gulf, India and the USA.

RIGHT: Air Tanzania 767-260ER ET-AIZ on lease from Ethiopian Airlines on final approach to London Gatwick. *Bruce Malcolm*

BELOW: China Southern use their three 767-300s for the routes around the Asian region. Boeing 767-31BER B-2566 leased from ILFC is seen on approach to Hong Kong Kai Tak in April 1998. *Philip Birtles*

Ethiopean Airlines took delivery of their first increased gross weight (345,000lb/156,489kg) 767-200ER when it arrived at Addis Ababa on 1 June 1984, the 7,500 mile (12,070) delivery flight from Washington DC, being the longest made to date by a twin engine airliner, (later beaten by the delivery to Kuwait Airways already mentioned). The aircraft carried 58 passengers over the 13 hour 17 minute flight and remained within the ICAO 90-minute overwater guidelines throughout the journey, as approval had not been given for full ETOPS at this stage. The successful Ethiopian Airways operated three 767-200s by 1996, and were considering a fleet rationalisation with the addition of two more 767-300s to help improve the cargo capacity.

In July 1984 the New Zealand Government gave approval of the first three 767-200ERs for the national airline, Air New Zealand. Powered by the GE CF6-80A2 engines developing 50,000lb (222 kN) thrust the aircraft were configured for 220 seats in a mixed class layout. Deliveries were scheduled for September 1985, March and September 1986. The first aircraft, ZK-NBA was handed over on 3 September 1985 with services commencing 12 days later gradually building up on the routes from Wellington–Singapore and to Tokyo, and Christchurch–Honolulu. In January 1987 a further 767-200ER was ordered. Under special rights granted by the Australian Government, Air New Zealand were permitted to fly up to five flights per week from Sydney–Los Angeles from November 1994, adding Sydney–Bangkok a year later. The carrier had already developed Brisbane as a regional hub for 767 operations to Osaka, Seoul, Taipei, Bangkok and New Zealand.

CAAC, the airline of the People's Republic of China ordered two P&W JT9D-7R4E4 powered 767-200ERs on 23 May 1985, later increasing their order by four more aircraft. The first aircraft, B-2551 was delivered on 8 October 1985, entering service soon after, and a further four P&W PW4052 powered 767s were ordered by CAAC in mid-1990. With the commercialisation of the Chinese airline operation, a number of domestic airlines were formed, and the CAAC 767s were taken over by Air China, with 767-300s being added to the fleet carrying a similar livery but with different titles.

LAN-Chile acquired two GE CF6-80A2 powered 767-200ERs from the International Lease Finance Corporation (ILFC) in February 1986 to replace two DC-10s in mid-1986 on the Santiago–Miami–New York service, with some extensions to European destinations. A further penetration of the South American market was made with the order for six GE CF6-80C2 powered 767-200ERs from Varig of Brazil on 18 March 1986. The total value of the order including four options was around $400 million and the new derivative of the CF-6 engine gave a range increase of up to 6,150 statute miles (11,390km) with a full payload of 200 passengers, the deliveries were scheduled to commence in May 1987, with the remainder of the firm orders by the end of the year. TACA of El Salvador ordered one 767 which was delivered on 22 May 1986, but to start services earlier until their own aircraft was delivered a 767 was leased from 1 October 1985.

In July 1986, the Charlotte NC based US domestic airline, Piedmont ordered six 767-200s with options on a further six powered by GE CF6-80C2 engines, as their first wide bodied aircraft, to start international operations. Deliveries commenced in May 1987 and they were put into service on the transatlantic operations, starting with London Gatwick, and other long range services. The airline was acquired by US Air in March 1987, but due to legal problems it took a year for the full merger to be completed. Three more 767-200s were ordered in April 1989 by US Air for the expanding ex-Piedmont operation, but some of the deliveries were delayed until 1990. These aircraft were then painted in BA livery, retaining the US registration, when BA and US Air proposed joint operations, but US Air pulled out when BA began to work with American Airlines on new joint proposals.

In April 1987, Lauda Air placed the launch order for the 56,000lb (250kN)thrust PW4000 powered 767-300ER for non-stop flights from the Vienna base to Bangkok, with the possibility of continuing on to Sydney or Beijing. Lauda Air had been having a battle with the Austrian Government for some years to be allowed to compete with the state owned Austrian Airlines on international scheduled services. The route licence was finally awarded in October 1987 with services to commence on 29 April 1988, and a second aircraft was ordered for a 1989 delivery. The first 767-300ER was delivered on 2 May 1988, and was soon put into service twice weekly to Bangkok, and once a week each to Hong Kong and Sydney. A 767-300 was ordered in September 1990 for use on European high density charter operations. Lauda Air added a further 767-300ER when an aircraft on lease from Ansett was delivered on 22 August 1995.

With both the P&W and GE engines powering the 767, in March 1987 an agreement was reached between Boeing and Rolls-Royce to consider fitting the 60,600lb (267kN) thrust RB524-D4D engines to the 767. As a result BA placed an order in August 1987 for 11 767-300s with options on a further 15 worth $500 million, the engines being similar to those powering the BA 747-400s. Deliveries were scheduled to commence at the end of 1989, and although the aircraft were to be allocated to the higher density European routes, as experience built up with the airframe/engine combination extended range over water operations would become possible. In October 1988 BA converted six of their options and added a further six 767s on option.

Canadian placed an initial order for six GE-powered 767-300ERs in April 1987, soon adding two more -300ERs with options for another 16. Two 767-200ERs were added in January 1988 with options on a further eight, and in October 1988 two of the options for the -300ERs were converted to firm commitments.

Rumours that Gulf Air were to lease a pair of 767-300s were confirmed in March 1988 for use on the carrier's long haul routes to the USA, Australia and Japan. The first 767-300 was delivered from Seattle to Bahrain on 20 June 1988, a distance of 8,085 miles (13,012km) in an elapsed time of 14hr 13min. In August, Gulf Air decided to purchase direct four 767s to replace their Tristar fleet, and in April 1989 ordered six 767-300ERs with options on 12 more. However, as a result of the economic problems caused by the aftermath of the Gulf War, Gulf Air disposed of some of their 767s, bringing some of the Tristars out of storage for the 1997 season, until the economy improved and they were finally able to replace the Tristars with 767s.

During 1988 sales of the Boeing 767 began to pick-up significantly, SAS starting the year with an order in January for nine 767s with options on 15 worth about $1.8 billion for the transatlantic routes commencing in March 1989. The firm orders were for seven -300ERs configured to carry 209 passengers in a two class layout on ranges up to 6,900 miles (11,104km), and two -200ERs carrying up to 150 passengers in two classes up to 7,200 miles (11,587km). The aircraft were to be powered by the PW4000 engines, and the 767s were selected in preference to the MD-11 and A340 because of the earlier availability. The first three 767-300ERs were allocated to the services from Scandinavia to New York and Chicago, later replacing earlier types of aircraft on the routes to Seattle, Los Angeles, Bangkok, Singapore, Hong Kong and Beijing. The capacity and range of the 767-200ERs was more suited to the less popular services to Tokyo and Rio de Janeiro. Four more 767-300ERs were ordered in early 1989, followed by another three at the end of the year.

Also in January, the German charter airline, LTU ordered three 767-300s worth $205 million and powered by the PW4000 engines, the first aircraft due for delivery the following January. Martinair of Holland also placed an order for two PW4000 powered 767-300ERs in the same month.

Boeing achieved another long distance record with the delivery flight of the first 767-200ER to Air Mauritius on 18 April 1988, flying the delivery leg of 8,727 miles (14,044km) from Halifax, Nova Scotia at an average speed of 460kt (853km/hr). The take off weight was 349,212lb (158,400kg) including 73 tonnes of fuel, and it landed with seven tonnes remaining, enough for a further two hours of flight. The Air Mauritius 767s were configured for 203 passengers in a three class layout, and optimised for the 13-hour non-stop flight to London. After the arrival of the second aircraft, services commenced in May bringing new destinations in Europe and Asia within non-stop flying time with the remote Indian Ocean Island, as well as serving destinations in the African continent. One 767-200ER was ordered by Air Zimbabwe in August 1988 with options on a further two powered by 56,750lb (254kN) thrust PW4056 engines. One options was converted in April 1989 for delivery in August 1990. The 767s were allocated to the Harare–London services, later removing the first class seats and improving the tourist layout to increase the passenger loads with a more spacious pitch and a 2-3-2 layout for the 10 hour

RIGHT: Japan Asia Airways 767-346 JA8987 leased from JAL on final approach over the busy city traffic at Hong Kong Kai Tak in April 1998. *Philip Birtles*

flight. The 767s are also used to provide a business express service to Nairobi and Johannesburg.

The 767-300 had become the most popular variant with 107 sold by October 1988, of which 56 were the extended range version. Total 767 sales stood at 307 aircraft, with 236 already delivered.

With the easing of political relations in Eastern Europe, LOT of Poland became the first of the former ex-Iron-Curtain countries to select western airline equipment. In November 1988 they selected two 767-200ERs and one -300ER powered by the GE CF6-80C2 engines to be flown on routes from Warsaw to New York, Chicago and Bangkok, with deliveries scheduled for the second quarter of 1989. Avianca of Columbia ordered two PW4000 powered 767-200ERs at the end of 1988 to enter service a year later on routes to Mexico City and destinations in the USA. For those airlines who did not wish to have the capital cost of the aircraft on their books, the lease operators kept their stocks up with nine more -300ERs for ILFC at the end of 1988 together with Ansett Worldwide who ordered six -300ERs together with some 757s. By the end of the year a total of 82 767s had been sold by Boeing in the previous 12 months. Orders continued to be achieved for the 767 from a mix of the smaller operator to the major carriers who kept their fleet topped up as their routes expanded. Amongst the smaller operators were Asiana of Korea who ordered two -300s early in 1989; Aero Maritime, the charter subsidiary of UTA, who ordered two -200ERs and one -300ER for delivery to start in September 1990 and Air Algerie who ordered three -300s worth $264 million for service entry in 1990. Amongst the major carriers were orders from Varig for four -300ERs worth £300 million; 16 -300s with 16 options from United in May 1989 to be powered by the PW4000 engines and 10 more -300s with a further 10 options in June from ANA. This made ANA potentially the largest 767 operator with 35 aircraft in service and five to be delivered, before this latest order. Two more 767-300s were ordered in October 1992, bringing their total commitment to 63 767s with the 50th aircraft delivered earlier in the month.

The Boeing 767 delivery flights continued to establish long distance records for twin jets with the first 767-200ER to Air Seychelles on 27 July 1989. The 8,892-mile (14,311km) flight was flown from Grand Rapids in Michigan to Mahe in the Indian Ocean. The 767 was used on the London, Frankfurt, Paris, Rome and Zurich routes, and a 767-300 was leased from ILFC from late 1996 to replace the airline's 757, which had become too small for the operators developing services. Evergreen of Taiwan ordered four 767-300ERs in October 1989 for delivery in early 1992, followed by Aer Lingus who ordered two 767-300ERs for their Shannon to Los Angeles services due to commence in 1991.

The first Rolls-Royce RB211-524G-powered 767-300 was rolled out at Everett in April 1989, commencing the flight test programme on 23 May. CAA clearance was achieved in July and full certification of the 60,600lb (267kN) thrust 524H engine was awarded in November ready for delivery to BA. The first four aircraft were configured for the European short haul routes with services commencing in early 1990, and these were followed soon after by four more aircraft configured with a three class layout for the Middle Eastern services.

Not long after the 767s entered service with BA, problems were experienced with cracks in the engine pylon supporting the one tonne heavier Rolls-Royce engines when compared with the P&W and GE powered aircraft. The cracks, up to 33cm long, were found in 767s which had flown between 250 and 1,000hr, the high time aircraft also having achieved the highest cycles with 1,100 landings on the London–Paris route. The aircraft were grounded from 23 August for temporary repairs pending a redesign to overcome the problem of the concentration of stress in a limited area. Further repairs were required a year later before the problem was finally cured.

The first of two 767-200ERs leased from Ansett International by Royal Brunei set new speed and endurance records on the delivery flight in June 1990 despite fuel burn problems with the PW4056 engines. The aircraft departed Seattle with a fuel load of 76.5 tonnes of high density JP-5 fuel on 8 June, climbing to 37,000ft (11,278m) for a Mach 0.77 maximum endurance cruise speed. The aircraft arrived overhead Nairobi having achieved the great circle distance record of 8,040nm (14,890km). The aircraft landed with 2.3 tonnes of fuel remaining, which was equivalent to a further 30min, a reserve only permitted on a non revenue flight. As well as the distance record, the speed record was claimed with 450kt (835kph) in a time of 17 hours 22 minutes between Seattle–Nairobi, before the delivery was completed to Mombasa, ready to enter service on the Jeddah route

With the end of 1990 approaching the reduction in demand for airliners caused by the current economic depression was worsened by the Gulf War, when passengers showed a reluctance to fly. Orders continued to be achieved, LAM of Mozambique signing for two 767-200s and three 767-300s in August, followed by Air Pacific of Fiji with one -200ER in October. Airlines were still looking into the future, anticipating the upturn in the world economic situation with the ending of the Gulf War, Gulf Air ordering 12 more 767-300ERs worth $1.15 billion. However, by mid-1996 continued losses by Gulf Air required some rationalisation. Two of the carriers 767-300ERs were leased out to LOT and Ethiopean Airlines and seven had the seating capacity increased from 200 to 237 for use on higher density routes. The aim was to pull out of unprofitable and non strategic routes and focus on improving overall performance. By early 1997, Gulf Air decided to dispose of six of its 18 767-300ERs, which were bought by Delta, the first two being delivered in March, followed by the remainder by June.

EVA Air leased two more 767-300ERs to add to their existing order to allow the early start of daily services to Singapore, Bangkok, Kuala Lumpur and Seoul and ordered two more in February 1992. At the end of the year Delta added a further six 767-200s and four 767-300s for their domestic operations. Malev became the second East European airline to order the 767 when they signed for two 767-200s and one -300ER in February 1991 powered by GE CF6-80C2 engines. The -300ER was the first to be delivered in April 1992 for use on

European scheduled routes and charter flights to Japan and the USA. Air New Zealand added four more 767-300ERs with five options in March bringing total sales to 598 aircraft.

Out of a total of 252 jet airliners sold by Boeing in 1991, the 767 accounted for 72 aircraft, although the overall sales was reduced from a total of 543 airliners in 1990 due to the world economic depression. Amongst the orders announced at the close of the year were 10 more 767-300ERs for United worth some $800 million. TWA also leased three 767-200ERs with a requirement for further aircraft either to buy or lease to be used on transatlantic operations from the New York Kennedy hub. Linhas Aeras de Mozambique took delivery of the first of two 767-200ERs in January 1992 with the second aircraft being delivered by the end of the year.

In 1992 American Airlines had become the world's largest airline with a target fleet size of 670 aircraft by the end of the year, making 2,550 daily departures to nearly 200 destinations around the world. By August 1992 American Airlines operated 25 767-300ERs and 30 767-200s, of which 22 were -200ERs, the aircraft being dedicated to the development of the expanding long-haul international network. A further 16 -300ERs were on order at the time, for delivery of nine in 1993 and the remaining five in 1994. In addition American Airlines also held options on a further 767-300ERs, the majority of the -300ERs being on operating leases, although due to the poor economic situation further expansion plans had been delayed.

In the first nine months of 1992, Boeing sold only eight 767s, and in November announced plans to reduce production of the type from five a month, to four by November 1993. But the recession was worse than anticipated, and in January 1993 the decision was made to reduce further the 767 production to three a month from October with many redundancies expected.

In March 1993 the Air UK charter subsidiary Leisure International Airways announced plans to lease two 767-300ERs from ILFC for transatlantic operations to commence on 1 May. The trickle of new orders continued with two 767-300ERs for Fiji based Air Pacific to add to the 767-200ER already in service. Both aircraft were leased from ILFC, the first being delivered in September 1994, followed by the second in 1996 to be used on new services to Taiwan, Hong Kong, Los Angeles and Osaka. In early 1994 Aeroflot announced a lease deal with GPA for four 767-300ERs with the first aircraft delivered in April for use on the transatlantic services from Moscow to the USA starting on 10 July.

In early 1994 Boeing announced a 767 production rate increase from three to four aircraft a month, by which time 665 aircraft had been sold with 143 remaining to be delivered. Kazakhstan Airlines selected the PW4056 engines in February 1994 for their four 767-300ERs with options on two more, the deliveries being scheduled between 1995 and 1997. In mid-1994 KLM made the decision to exchange its fleet of 10 Airbus A.310-200s for seven 767-300ERs on lease from ILFC. Although the two types were hardly similar, the 767s gave dou-

BELOW: Air Canada leased 767-333ER C-FMWP to Polynesian, who used the aircraft for services to Sydney. *Andrew Briggs*

ble the range of the A.310s on European routes with 20 percent more fleet capacity, also allowing route expansion to include North America and the Middle East. The seven-year lease contract provided for an additional five aircraft and the aircraft were delivered between June 1995 and August 1996. The lease on three more 767-300ERs was confirmed in June 1995, the first being delivered the following month. Another lease deal in mid-1994 was one 767-300ER to Sobelair, the charter subsidiary of Sabena for use on long range routes to Thailand, Sri Lanka, Mombasa and Dominica. The aircraft was supplied on a two-year lease from Ansett of Australia.

The leasing of a number of 767s to the airlines helped to reduce the stocks of the leasing companies, but there was a need for direct sales to revitalise the production line. The order from Britannia Airways for four GE CF6-80C2 powered 767-300ERs with options on a further four aircraft in November 1994 was therefore welcome. The firm order aircraft were for delivery in 1996 to be added to the nine 767-200s already in service on charter flights to destinations as far away as Australia, the new aircraft giving increased capacity. In early 1995 Rolls-Royce won their second order for the RB211-524H to power the 767 when China Yunnan selected the engines for three 767-300s and options on a further three. The first aircraft was for delivery in May 1996 with the other two following in June and then January 1997. The new aircraft entered service on long-haul and domestic services from the Kunming base in Yunnan Province, and this order brought total sales of the 767 to 690 aircraft.

However, a number of major airlines were still suffering from economic problems, Continental admitting to discussions with Boeing about delivery delays and in January 1995 Air France were threatening to cancel all their outstanding orders with Airbus and Boeing. A compromise agreement was reached with Boeing in May where the seven 767-300ERs previously ordered would be replaced by a later order for three 767-300ERs, and a single 767-300 delivered in 1994 but not put into service was sold by Boeing. This was part of an overall deal involving 737-400s and a 747-400C. Two of the original allocation to Air France were sold to Royal Brunei with delivery in March and April 1996 taking the total fleet to nine 767-300s, but because they were powered by the GE engines, rather than having commonality with the remainder of the P&W powered fleet, they became difficult to support, and the decision was made to dispose of them in September 1997.

Three new build 767-300ERs were leased to Alitalia in August 1995 by Singapore Aircraft Leasing Enterprise (SALE) in conjunction with Ansett Worldwide Aviation Services. The first aircraft was delivered in early August, with the other two following in November and February 1996, joining two other 767s leased by Alitalia in early 1995. Monarch Airlines operate the aircraft on behalf of the Italian airline.

Vietnam Airlines were operating three 767-300ERs and one 767-200ER on wet leases from AWAS and Royal Brunei Airlines in 1995, and were preparing to dry lease from GE Capital Aviation Services (GECAS) three ex-Continental 767-300ERs to replace the earlier aircraft from early 1996.

Meanwhile, the Manchester based Airtours International had plans to introduce a pair of 767-300ERs and six 757s for the 1996 summer season, as part of their fleet rationalisation with the replacement of the earlier MD-83s with Airbus A320s.

On 1 March Boeing delivered their 8,000th commercial jet airliner when a 767-300ER was handed over to KLM, the first 707 being handed over to PanAm in August 1958. Transaero, a Russian independent airline were investigating the options of leasing three or four 767s in March 1996 to add to their fleet of 737s and 757s to cover anticipated route expansion. A decision was finally made a year later when the lease of three 767-200ERs was agreed for the P&W JT9D powered ex-Egyptair aircraft which were originally delivered in 1984. The first of the 767s was delivered in June allowing a start to be made on the planned Moscow–New York service.

The airliner market began to show signs of improvement during the first half of 1996 although much of this was due to switching of types, the major item being Delta exchanging 52 737-300s for 12 767-300ERs, while Irish lessor GPA was still fighting for survival, shedding eight 767s amongst other aircraft. In the first six months the 767 had gained seven net orders with 20 aircraft delivered, and a healthy backlog of 105 aircraft. The major gains for Boeing were for the new generation 737s and the new 777. Perhaps the most significant event to signify the growing maturity of the 767 was the debut of the type in the ageing airline census with the first aircraft passing the 15 years in service, mainly the early models in service with United which had entered service in August 1982.

By September 1996 220 767-200s were in operation with none due for delivery, and 385 -300s with 85 further on order, the most popular version being the 767-300ER. By the end of 1996 overall net airliner orders exceeded the 1,000 mark for the first time in nearly a decade, although it was the new generation aircraft which achieved the best results. The net orders for the 767 was for 12 aircraft with 44 deliveries which included two new 767-200ERs to be configured as AWACS for Japan.

From humble beginnings in 1989 the privately owned Asiana Airlines began to break the monopolistic stranglehold of the national carrier Korean Airlines in early 1997. The fleet already included 12 767-300ERs with two orders and two options to be confirmed. In addition Asiana operated one freighter version with a further example to join the fleet in 1998. Reaching a peak of 18 767-300ERs in 1998 and 1999, the 767 fleet will be reduced gradually from 2000 as additional capacity is acquired with the delivery of the larger A330s and Boeing 777s.

An encouraging but modest sale was for three 767-300ERs worth $300 million to LanChile in mid-1997, the airline already operating 10 earlier aircraft on various operating leases. The CF6-80C2 powered aircraft were ordered to provide additional international passenger and cargo capacity and the first was delivered in April 1998. British Airways also topped up their 767-300 fleet with three additional aircraft ordered in mid-1997 at the same time as options were confirmed on five more 777-200s. The deliveries of the new 767-300s were made in April and May 1998, and were probably amongst the first of

the type to be painted in the new colours. A more substantial order came from United at the end of June for eight 767-300ERs for delivery starting in May 1998 and completed in 2000. Citybird, the Belgian low fare scheduled airline decided to acquire two 268 seat 767-300ERs in July 1997 for delivery in February and March 1998. Both aircraft are leased from Ansett Worldwide Aviation Services, the first coming straight off the Everett production line, and the second being a 1996 built example previously leased to Vietnam Airlines.

As a positive indication of the improved airline business, ILFC placed orders for 126 new airliners in September 1997, shared almost equally between Airbus and Boeing. Amongst the Boeing order were seven 767-300ERs and five of the new stretched 767-400ERs, details of which will be covered in a separate chapter. Total sales of the 767s had reached 654, of which 434 were the 767-300, with 71 backlog of deliveries. Soon after Delta placed a sole supplier deal with Boeing which included 10 orders and 10 options for GE CF6-80C2 powered 767-300/300ERs as well as the launch order for the 767-400ER.

With the rapidly growing demand for Boeing airliners, and the pressures of developing the 737 and 777 family, the company experienced a number of supplier difficulties in the latter half of 1997, which were not resolved during the first half of 1998. Even the well established 767 line was effected, which caused the Japanese start up airline Hokkaido International to defer the launch of their regular services due to the non availability of a new build 767-300ER leased from Ansett which was running about two months late.

In April 1998 Air Madagascar phased out its sole Boeing 747 and replace it with a 767-300ER leased from GE Capital until the delivery of a new aircraft in April 1999. Similarly Air Namibia replaced their sole 747SP with an ex-Challenge Air 767-300ER which entered service on 1 April 1998 on routes to Frankfurt and London Heathrow. The German charter operator, LTU also decided to reduce some of its long range routes to Asia and the USA in the winter of 1998, disposing of the four MD-11s to Swissair, and replacing them with two more 767-300ERs, to bring their total fleet of this type to seven aircraft.

With a healthy backlog of orders for the current 767-300ER, including top-ups from existing operators, and excellent prospects for the stretched 767-400ER, the Boeing 767 is set to be in volume production well into the next century, no doubt more than paying for its original development programme and earning Boeing some significant profits even in today's highly competitive world airline markets.

In May 1998 the 701st 767 was ready for delivery, in this case to American Airlines, with further 767-300s on the production line for ANA and JAL. With the new developments and orders in hand, the aircraft looks set to continue in production well into the next century, and could well achieve a total run of over 1,000 aircraft.

# 6 CUSTOMERS

## AER LINGUS

Aer Lingus ordered two 767-300ERs in October 1989, followed later by two more for the services from Shannon–Los Angeles. Aer Lingus 767-3Y0ER EI-CAL was the first to be delivered, and is seen taking off from Everett. It was later operated by Aeromexico as XA-RWW, and is now in service with TWA.
*Boeing*

## AEROFLOT

CENTRE LEFT: In early 1994 Aeroflot announced a lease with GPA for four 767-300ERs for use between Moscow and the USA. The first aircraft was 767-3Y0ER EI-CKD and is seen on approach to London Heathrow in October 1997. *Nick Granger*

## AÉROMARITIME

LEFT: Aéromaritime was the charter subsidiary of the French independent second force airline UTA, which was later taken over by Air France. Aéromaritime ordered two 767-200ERs and one 767-300ER for delivery to commence in September 1990. The first aircraft for Aéromaritime, 767-27AER F-GHGD is seen taking off from Everett, and is now leased to Balkan. *Boeing*

## AIR CANADA

BOTTOM LEFT: First deliveries outside the USA were to Air Canada in October 1982 who had placed an initial order for 10 767-200s. Air Canada 767-233ER C-GDSP powered by the P&W JT9D-7R4D engines is seen on finals to London Heathrow in April 1992. *Philip Birtles*

BELOW: Air Canada placed a further order for nine 767-200ERs to replace Tristars on the transatlantic routes. Air Canada 767-233ER C-GDSY in the new colours is seen ready for departure from London Heathrow in April 1997. *Philip Birtles*

BOTTOM: Air Canada placed an order for nine 767-300s in August 1989, although the fleet now consists of six of this variant. Air Canada 767-333ER C-FMXC in the new livery is awaiting instructions to enter the runway for departure from Heathrow in April 1997. *Philip Birtles*

## AIR MAURITIUS

FAR LEFT: The delivery flight of the Air Mauritius 767-200ER on 18 April 1988 created another long distance speed record. The aircraft flew non stop, the 8,727 miles/14,044km from Halifax Nova Scotia–Mauritius at an average speed of 460kt/853km/h. Air Mauritius 767-23BER 3B-NAK was the first of two -200ERs, and later a 767-300ER was added. *Boeing*

## AIR EUROPE ITALY

LEFT: Air Europe Italy took delivery of their first 767-35HER I-AEJD on 14 August 1992. It was later registered S7-AAQ and then returned to Air Europe as EI-CJA. *Boeing*

## AIR NEW ZEALAND

BELOW LEFT: Air New Zealand 767-319ER ZK-NCL flew from Everett–Christchurch New Zealand setting a new non stop world speed record, completing the 6,627 nm/ 12,273km in just under 15 hours. *Boeing*

## AIR SEYCHELLES

BELOW: The second 767 ordered by Air Seychelles was a 767-3Q8ER S7-AHM *Vailee de Mai* on lease from ILFC and seen visiting London Gatwick in February 1998. *Nick Granger*

### AIR SEYCHELLES

MAIN PICTURE: The delivery flight of the Air Seychelles 767-200ER broke another non stop long distance record on 27 July 1989. The aircraft flew the 14,311km (7,727 nm) from Grand Rapids in Michigan–Mahe. The sole Air Seychelles 767-2Q8ER S7-AAS was bought to replace the earlier 757, as increased capacity was required on the services to Europe. *Boeing*

### AIR ZIMBABWE

INSET RIGHT: Air Zimbabwe ordered one 767-200ER in August 1988, followed later by a second aircraft. These aircraft fly from Harare–London Gatwick. Air Zimbabwe 767-2N0ER Z-WPE *Victoria Falls*, the first for the airline, is seen taking off from Everett. *Boeing*

### AIRTOURS INTERNATIONAL

INSET LEFT: The Manchester based Airtours International introduced a pair of 767-300ERs for the 1996 summer season, 767-31KER G-DIMB visiting London Gatwick in June 1997. *Nick Granger*

ABOVE RIGHT: Aircraft tend to change hemispheres for the changing busy seasons. When it is busy in Europe, it is quieter in Australasia, and Airtours leased 767-35HER ZK-NCM from Air New Zealand for the 1998 summer season. It is seen here at London Gatwick on a rather unseasonable day in July 1998. *Philip Birtles*

## ALITALIA

BELOW: Singapore Aircraft Leasing (SALE) leased three new build 767-300ERs to Alitalia in August 1995 to be operated by Monarch Airlines crews. Alitalia Team 767-33AER I-DEID/G-OITC is seen departing from London Heathrow in February 1998. *Nick Granger*

## AMERICAN AIRLINES

BELOW RIGHT: American Airlines also specified the GE CF6-80 engines for the initial order for 30 767s, plus options on a further 32. The first delivery was on 4 November 1982 with seating for up to 24 first class and 180 economy class passengers. The highly polished American 767-223ER N336AA is seen on approach to London Heathrow in June 1997. *Philip Birtles*

ABOVE: American Airlines 767s have also operated into Manchester as an important UK gateway. American 767-223ER N332AA is ready for push-back at Manchester in October 1987. *Philip Birtles*

MAIN PICTURE: Following the initial order for 30 767-200s, all further orders by American Airlines have been for the 767-300 version. New American 767-323ER N39367 is seen taking off from Paine Field at Everett. *Boeing*

ABOVE: American Airlines has also operated flights into London Gatwick with the 767s. American 767-323ER N369AA is seen ready for departure from Gatwick in August 1995. *Philip Birtles*

ABOVE LEFT: By 1992, American Airlines had become the world's largest airline operating a large fleet of 767-200s, 767-200ERs and 767-300ERs totalling 55 aircraft with more on order. American 767-323ER N367AA is seen on approach to Orlando in August 1988. *Philip Birtles*

## ALL NIPPON AIRWAYS

FAR LEFT: All Nippon Airways ordered 10 767-300s in June 1989 with 10 options to add to the 35 767s already in service, with five more to be delivered. ANA 767-381 JA8258 is just about to touch down. *ANA*

LEFT: All Nippon Airways are potentially the largest 767 operator with a fleet of at least 63 aircraft, and the 50th aircraft delivered in October 1992. The fleet consisted of a mix of 767-200s and -300s, and one of the -200s was ANA 767-281 JA8490, which has now been sold to Airborne Express for conversion to the cargo configuration. *ANA*

## ANSETT AUSTRALIA

CENTRE LEFT: The first 767-200 of five ordered by Ansett Australia was delivered in June 1983. Ansett 767-277 VH-RME, now one of seven of the type operating with the airline, is seen about to land at Sydney–Mascot in December 1992. *Philip Birtles*

## ASIANA

BOTTOM LEFT: Asiana of South Korea ordered their first two 767-300ERs in early 1989. Asiana 767-38EER HL7263 was the first of what was to become a fleet of 10 aircraft, and is seen taking off from Everett. *Boeing*

## AVIANCA

BELOW: Avianca Columbia ordered two 767-200ERs at the end of 1988 for services to Mexico City and destinations in the USA. Avianca 767-259ER N985AN is seen in the specially developed paint shop at Everett. *Boeing*

## BALKAN BULGARIAN

BELOW: Boeing 767-27AER F-GHGD. *Balkan*

## BRITANNIA AIRWAYS

FAR LEFT: Britannia was the first to put the 767 into British service. The first of the initial order for 767-200s was delivered to the airline at London Luton Airport in February 1984. Britannia 767-204 G-BKVZ was one of the original batch and is seen at Luton before going to Ansett Australia as VH-RMK. This aircraft does not have an observation deck above the cabin. *Philip Birtles*

CENTRE LEFT: Britannia Airways used the 767-200s for the high density more popular holiday charter flights throughout Europe. Britannia 767-204 G-BKPW is seen turning at the end of the runway at Rhodes ready to take more holiday makers home in September 1995. This aircraft has now been leased to Ansett Australia as VH-RML. *Philip Birtles*

LEFT: Britannia Airways placed an order for four CF6-80C2 powered 767-300ERs in November 1994 with options on another four, later confirmed. Britannia 767-304ER G-OBYB, the second delivered, is seen ready to depart from a windy Rhodes runway in August 1997. *Philip Birtles*

**BRITISH AIRWAYS**

RIGHT: Although BA operates the 767-300ERs across the North Atlantic services, they are also used for the more busy European routes. BA 767-336ER G-BNWK *City of Amsterdam* is ready for departure from Heathrow in October 1994 with the title 'Fly New Club Europe' along the roof.

*Philip Birtles*

LEFT: While British Airways prepared for the launch of the new image, any aircraft due for a repaint was finished in an interim scheme. BA 767-336ER G-BNWH *City of Brussels* is seen at Gatwick with the interim scheme in October 1997. *Nick Granger*

ABOVE: Britannia Airways 767-304ER G-OBYE with 'Keep Duty Free' titles at London Gatwick in July 1998. *Philip Birtles*

INSET LEFT: The combination of the 767-300 with Rolls-Royce RB211-524G engines was certificated by the CAA in November 1989 ready for deliveries to commence to BA. BA 767-336ER G-BNWB *City of Paris* was the second aircraft of the order and is seen at London Heathrow in August 1990. *Philip Birtles*

## CAAC

ABOVE: CAAC of China placed the initial order for two P&W powered 767-200s in May 1985 with the first delivery on 8 October. Later 767-300s were also ordered. With the commercialisation of Chinese airlines, six 767-200ERs and four 767-300ERs were taken over by Air China. Air China 767-3J6ER B-2557, the first of the 767-300s is seen at Singapore in November 1992. *Philip Birtles*

## CANADIAN AIRLINES INTERNATIONAL

MAIN PICTURE: Canadian Airlines International placed its initial order for six GE-powered 767-300ERs in April 1987. Canadian continued to increase its 767 fleet, both with -300ERs and -200ERs. Amongst other routes, the 767-300ERs were used on the North Atlantic services. The first aircraft, 767-375ER C-FCAB is seen on a delivery test flight. *Boeing*

## CONDOR

RIGHT: Condor, the German charter operator, currently operates a fleet of nine 767-300ERs. ILFC lease Boeing 767-330ER D-ABUX is seen departing from Rhodes in October 1993. *Philip Birtles*

## DELTA AIR LINES

FAR RIGHT: The second 767 customer was Delta who specified GE CF6-80 engines to power the initial order of 20 aircraft. The first for Delta, 767-232 N101DA was the sixth aircraft off the production line, and was used in the development flying of the different airframe/engine combination. *Boeing*

ABOVE: Delta Air Lines later also added the stretched 767-300s to its large fleet by placing the initial order on 21 February 1984. Delta 767-332 N127DL is seen moving towards the departure point at Orlando in August 1988. *Philip Birtles*

## EL AL
ABOVE: El Al initiated 767 services in Europe with a flight from London–Tel Aviv in July 1983. El Al 767-258  4X-EAB is the second of two 767-200s, followed by a pair of 767-200ERs. *Philip Birtles*

## ETHIOPIAN AIRLINES
BELOW: Ethiopian Airlines took delivery of the first of two 767-200ERs at Addis Ababa on 1 June 1984. Ethiopian 767-260ER ET-AIE, the first aircraft to be delivered to the airline is seen on the BA apron at London Heathrow in January 1989. *Philip Birtles*

## EVERGREEN
BOTTOM RIGHT: Evergreen of Taiwan-Eva Air, ordered four 767-300ERs in October 1989, and 767-3T7ER B-16601 was the first to be delivered. *Boeing*

## GULF AIR
RIGHT: The first 767-300ER was delivered to Gulf Air on 20 June 1988, covering the distance of 8,085 miles (13,011km) non-stop from Seattle–Bahrain in an elapsed time of 14 hours 13 minutes. Gulf Air 767-3P6ER A40-GF was the first aircraft delivered, and has since been sold to TransBrasil as PT-TAL. *Boeing*

LEFT: Gulf Air uses the 767-300ERs for services to Asia. Gulf Air 767-3P6ER A40-GY is seen on final approach to Hong Kong Kai Tak in April 1998. *Philip Birtles*

BELOW LEFT: Due to economic difficulties in 1997, Gulf Air disposed of some of its 767-300ERs and brought instead some stored Tristars out of retirement. The 767s were also used to fly to European destinations, and Gulf Air 767-3P6ER A40-GW is ready for departure at London Heathrow in August 1994. *Philip Birtles*

BELOW: By early 1997 Gulf Air decided to dispose of six of the 767-300ERs to Delta Air Lines. Gulf Air 767-3P6ER A40-GJ is seen on approach to London Heathrow in June 1997. *Philip Birtles*

## JAPAN AIRLINES
BOTTOM: Japan Airlines is a major operator of the Boeing 767, both the -200 and -300, the initial order being placed in September 1983 for four 767-200s and two 767-200ERs. JAL 767-246 JA8233 is taxiing to the departure point at Hong Kong Kai Tak in April 1998. *Philip Birtles*

FAR LEFT: Japan Airlines also placed the launch order for the Boeing 767-300 in September 1983 for high density routes around the Asian region. JAL 767-346 JA8264 is seen on final approach to Hong Kong Kai Tak in April 1998. *Philip Birtles*

## KLM

BOTTOM LEFT: In mid-1994 KLM decided to replace its fleet of Airbus A310s with 767-300ERs leased from ILFC. KLM 767-306ER PH-BZE was the fifth in the batch of 11 aircraft covered by the lease, and is seen on approach to London Heathrow in May 1998. *Philip Birtles*

## KUWAIT AIRWAYS

BELOW: Kuwait Airways ordered three 767-200s in September 1984, but with the invasion of Kuwait by Iraq, two were flown to Baghdad where they were destroyed in air attacks in February 1991, the surviving aircraft being sold. Kuwait Airways 767-269ER 9K-AIB was one of the two destroyed, and is seen in better days on approach to London Heathrow. *Philip Birtles*

## LAUDA AIR

MAIN PICTURE: Lauda Air placed the launch order for the PW4000-powered 767-300ER in April 1997 for non-stop flights from Vienna to Bangkok, and followed soon after with an order for another aircraft. The first 767-3Z9ER OE-LAU *Marilyn Monroe* was delivered on 2 May 1988. *Boeing*

BELOW: As the Lauda fleet of 767s grew to five aircraft, the aircraft were allocated to other routes including European inclusive tours. Lauda Air 767-3Z9ER OE-LAU is seen at Rhodes in August 1997 taking aboard another batch of departing holiday makers. *Philip Birtles*

## LEISURE INTERNATIONAL
FAR RIGHT: Leisure International leased two 767-300ERs from ILFC for transatlantic operations commencing on 1 May 1993. Leisure 767-39HER G-UKLI is seen ready for departure from London Gatwick in August 1995. *Philip Birtles*

## LOT
RIGHT: LOT of Poland ordered a pair of 767-200ERs in November 1988, together with one 767-300ER. It later increased its order for 767-300ERs to three aircraft. LOT 767-35DER SP-LPA *Warsaw* is seen taking off from Paine Field at Everett. *Boeing*

## LTU

ABOVE: In January 1988 the German charter operator LTU ordered three PW.4000 powered 767-300ERs for delivery the following January, to be used on North Atlantic inclusive tours. LTU Sud 767-3G5ER D-AMUN was the first of an eventual fleet of six aircraft. *Boeing*

## MALEV

RIGHT: Malev became the second East European airline to specify the Boeing 767, when two were ordered in February 1991 powered by the CF6-80C2 engines. Malev 767-27GER HA-LHA, on lease from GPA, is seen on approach to London Heathrow in August 1998. *Philip Birtles*

## MARTINAIR

FAR RIGHT: Martinair of Holland placed an order for two PW4000-powered 767-300ERs in January 1988. Martinair used the 767-300ERs for holiday charter to a number of destinations. Martinair 767-31AER PH-MCG, the first aircraft, is seen taking off from Paine Field at Everett. *Boeing*

## PIEDMONT

RIGHT: Piedmont ordered six 767-200ERs in July 1986, starting international services to Gatwick in May 1987. The first Piedmont 767-201ER, N603P is seen at Gatwick in December 1987. *Philip Birtles*

ABOVE: In March 1987 Piedmont was acquired by US Air and the six 767-200ERs were painted in the new livery. US Air 767-201ER N647US (previously N607P with Piedmont) is seen on approach to London Gatwick. *Bruce Malcolm*

## QANTAS

LEFT INSET: Qantas placed an initial order for six 767-200s in September 1983 powered by JT9D engines followed by 13 CF6-80C2 engined 767-300s in May 1987. Qantas operate the 767-300s from Australia to a number of Asian destinations requiring the extended range capability. Qantas 767-338ER VH-OGJ is seen at Hong Kong Kai Tak awaiting departure clearance from the now closed airport.
*Philip Birtles*

## ROYAL BRUNEI

RIGHT: Royal Brunei leased two
767-200ERs from Ansett International
powered by PW4056 engines. Once
again a record was claimed for the
delivery flight, the distance of 8,040nm
(14,890km) from Seattle to overhead
Nairobi in a time of 17 hours 22 minutes.
Royal Brunei followed the order for the
767-200ERs with a batch of eight 767-
300ERs. The first 767-33AER
V8-RBF is seen moving off from the
ramp at Everett and two of the 767-300
fleet are leased to Japan Pacific Airlines.
*Boeing*

## SAS

ABOVE: Included in the January 1988
order for 767s by SAS was a pair of 767-
200ERs powered by the PW.4000
engines, and capable of carrying 150
passengers up to 7,200 miles (13,334km).
SAS 767-283ER LN-RCC is seen on
approach to London Heathrow in June
1993, and has since been sold to
TransBrasil as PT-TAJ. *Philip Birtles*

ABOVE RIGHT: The SAS 767-300ERs
operate on routes as far apart as Hong
Kong and Seattle. SAS 767-383ER
OY-KDO, previously registered
SE-DKT, is seen at Hong Kong Kai Tak
in April 1998 moving towards the
departure point. *Philip Birtles*

ABOVE INSET: In addition to the long-range routes, SAS also operate
767-300ERs on European services — such as can be seen here. SAS 767-383ER
OY-KDH is on approach to London Heathrow in June 1997. *Philip Birtles*

## SPANAIR

MAIN PICTURE: The Spanish charter operator Spanair, based in Mallorca, has a
pair of 767-300ERs in its fleet. Here one of its two Boeing 767-3YOERs, EC-FCU

*Baleares* on lease from GPA, is seen visiting London Gatwick in May 1997.
*Nick Granger*

## TACA

RIGHT INSET: TACA of El Salvador ordered its first 767-200 for delivery in May
1986, followed later by a 767-300ER. TACA 767-300ER N768TA is seen at London
Gatwick in January 1994. *Nick Granger*

## TRANSBRASIL

**BOTTOM LEFT:** TransBrasil is currently in the process of changing its aircraft colour scheme. Boeing 767-283ER PT-TAI, leased from SAS who registered it SE-DKP, is seen in the old livery at London Gatwick in April 1997. *Nick Granger*

## TWA

**MAIN PICTURE:** TWA took delivery of the first of 10 JT9D-7R4D powered 767-200s in November 1982, commencing commercial flight on 9 December. TWA 767-231ER N610TW is seen after arrival at Gatwick in July 1998. *Philip Birtles*

**ABOVE:** TWA are in the process of adopting a new livery. TWA 767-231ER N605TW, the fifth to be delivered to the airline, is seen at London Gatwick in September 1997. *Nick Granger*

## UNITED AIRLINES

MAIN PICTURE: United Airlines placed the launch order for 30 767-200s on 14 July 1978, specifying P&W JT9D-7R engines. The first aircraft was handed over to the airline on 19 August 1982 and commercial services were inaugurated on 8 September. United 767-222 N603UA was the fourth aircraft off the Everett production line, and participated in the development flying programme. *Boeing*

INSET LEFT: In 1989 United placed a further substantial order for 16 767-300ERs, with options on a further 16. United 767-322ER N643UA is seen ready for departure from London Heathrow in July 1995. *Philip Birtles*

INSET RIGHT: United later added 767-300ERs to the fleet, 767-322ER N654UA — still in the old colours — is seen on final approach to Hong Kong Kai Tak in April 1998. *Philip Birtles*

LEFT: In recent years United has been adopting a new livery for the aircraft. The initial order for 767-200s included normal range aircraft for US domestic routes, and extended range versions for international flights. United 767-222ER N606UA *City of Chicago* (the ninth aircraft off the production line) was the first to be delivered to the airline in August 1982. It is seen here ready for departure from London Heathrow in October 1994. *Philip Birtles*

BELOW: United 767-322ER N663UA is seen in the new colours on approach to London Heathrow in June 1997. *Philip Birtles*

## US AIR

BELOW LEFT: British Airways and US Air formed an uneasy partnership, and the 767-200s of US Air were painted in the BA livery. BA/US Air 767-2B7ER N654US is seen ready for departure from London Gatwick in August 1995. *Philip Birtles*

## US AIRWAYS

BELOW LEFT: With the break from the BA alliance, US Air took on a new image, becoming US Airways and adopting a new livery. US Airways 767-2B7ER N656US is one of a total of 12 with the airline and is seen at Gatwick in May 1998. *Nick Granger*

## UZBEKISTAN

ABOVE: A dramatic shot of Uzbekistan 767-300ER VP-BUA on final approach to London Gatwick in February 1998. *Nick Granger*

## VARIG

LEFT: Varig ordered six CF6-80C2 powered 767-200ERs, the first entering service in June 1987. Engine certification testing included a 5,790 st mile (9,318km) flight from Seattle to Bolivia, and tests at the 13,358ft (4,072m) altitude La Paz Airport. Varig 767-241 ER PP-VNO was the second aircraft for the airline. *Boeing*

BELOW: In March 1989 Varig ordered four 767-300ERs powered by CF6-80C2 engines. First delivery was 22 December 1989. Varig 767-341ER PP-VOJ was the second of this version delivered to the airline. *Nick Granger*

# 7 INCIDENTS AND ACCIDENTS

The Boeing 767 has an excellent safety record, but incidents and accidents have occurred. In the first year of operation the 767 escaped from two potentially serious incidents. The first was in late July 1983 when Air Canada 767 C-GUAN, carrying 61 passengers and eight crew, experienced fuel starvation. The fuel shortage began on the ground before departure, where the fuel tanks were physically checked with a dip-stick, due to the unservicability of the fuel quantity sensors. The error was made by reading the contents in kilogrammes instead of pounds, leading the pilots to believe that they had more than twice the fuel than was the actual case. The crew were first alerted to a problem with a low fuel pressure warning when cruising at 41,000ft (12,497m), and the captain elected to divert to Winnipeg. While descending through 31,000ft (9,449m), one engine stopped, followed by the second 3,000ft (914m) lower. An effort was made to provide electrical power by starting the APU, but as that also used aircraft fuel, it soon stopped. With the loss of hydraulic power, the ram air turbine dropped out to provide emergency power, and it soon became obvious that the aircraft would not be able to reach Winnipeg. An alternative — the disused air force base at Gimli — was selected, but it was no longer operational and had been converted to a motor racing circuit. The crew managed to maintain the aircraft in a glide for 60 miles (97km), taking 15 minutes, the captain using his sailplane skills to keep the aircraft in the air. It put down on the runway successfully, running through a number of metal barriers causing the nosewheel to collapse, and ending up at the end of the runway with no injuries to the occupants of the aircraft, or anyone on the ground. When the situation was tested on the flight simulator, the pilots lost control every time, confirming the skillful handling of the situation by the crew. The lesson learned from this incident, was that the 767 would not be allowed to operate with an unserviceable fuel contents system.

The second incident was also power related, and concerned a United Airlines 767 flying from Los Angeles–Denver on 19 August 1983, when during a descent from 41,000ft (12,497m), the captain shut down both engines, because he believed they were overheating. During the descent the aircraft entered cloud at 30,000ft (9,144m) and the power was increased to above idle to prevent engine icing. However, the main generators cut-out, leaving stand-by power and instruments only. The APU was started and the RAT was dropped out, and with the rise in exhaust gas temperatures the engines were stopped at 19,900ft (6,066m) and 17,400ft (5,304m), successful relights being made at 15,600ft (4,755m) and 14,500ft (4,420m). This was normal operating procedure, but it was not expected to lose both engines at the same time. The aircraft made a safe landing at its destination and the engines were removed for inspection, a likely contributory factor of the power loss being icing.

The first major accident to a 767 happened on 27 May 1991 to a Lauda Air 767-300ER 15 minutes after take-off from Bangkok. When the aircraft was climbing through around 26,000ft (7,925m) a sudden catastrophic failure caused the aircraft to crash killing all 223 people on board as it fell into the Thai jungle.

The suddenness of the disaster led to the usual speculation about a bomb, but after a painstaking and demanding investigation, the cause was found to be the uncommanded operation of the port engine reverse thrust. The sudden asymmetric loads were beyond the control capabilities of the pilots, and the aircraft turned over and dived towards the ground, shedding parts as it rapidly descended. Once the cause had been established, modifications were made to avoid any repetition, and meanwhile as a safety factor, the reverse thrust system was deactivated until the changes could be made.

Another serious accident was the hostile highjacking of Ethiopian Airlines 767-200ER ET-AIZ on 23 November 1996. Soon after take-off from Addis Ababa and established in the cruise for its destination of Nairobi, the aircraft was highjacked by three Ethiopian men who claimed to be carrying a bomb and demanded to be taken to Australia. The highjackers, whose motives never became clear, did not kill anyone directly, but used violence on the pilots. The crew eventually attempted a crash landing due to fuel exhaustion, ditching close to the Comoros Islands near Mozambique. The aircraft touched the water left wing low, breaking into three sections, the forward and centre sections turning over and sinking almost immediately. Of 12 crew and 163 passengers, 10 of the crew and 117 passengers were killed either by the impact or drowning.

During the approach to Dallas/Fort Worth on 27 March 1997 a Delta Air Lines 767 had an 18ft (5.5m) section of trailing edge outboard wing flap detached itself in flight, damaging the spoilers during separation. A safe landing was made, the resulting roll being controlled with the ailerons, but as a precaution, the FAA issued an emergency airworthiness directive (AD) requiring flap inspections within two weeks for 767s with more than 25,000 flying hours or 10,000 flight cycles. The AD required a torque check on the hinge fitting bolts on the outboard trailing edge flaps, the main carriers affected being Delta, American, United, Alaska Airlines and UPS. The bolts on the incident aircraft showed evidence of corrosion and fracture before the event.

The Boeing 767 has therefore proved to be a very safe aircraft to operate, more than justifying the two-crew operation on long range flights, often over featureless ocean, and its 'lack' of two engines has proved no inconvenience whatever.

# 8 CHRONOLOGY

| | |
|---|---|
| 14 July 1978 | Launch order for 30 P&W JT9D-7R4 powered 767s by United. |
| 14 Aug 1978 | Aeritalia became major risk sharing partner on 767. |
| 22 Sept 1978 | CTDC of Japan became major risk sharing partner in 767. |
| 15 Nov 1978 | American and Delta ordered 30 & 20 CF6 powered 767s. |
| 6 July 1979 | Fabrication of first parts at Boeing Auburn, Washington |
| 8 April 1981 | Final assembly of first 767 began at Everett |
| 4 Aug 1981 | Completion and roll-out of first 767. |
| 26 Sept 1981 | Maiden flight of 2hr 4min of first 767. |
| 27 May 1982 | Maiden flight of first 767 fitted with two-crew flightdeck. |
| July 1982 | First international demonstration tour to Europe, Africa and Mid East. |
| 30 July 1982 | Type certificate awarded by FAA. |
| 19 Aug 1982 | First 767 delivery to United Airlines. |
| 8 Sept 1982 | First 767 commercial service by United from Chicago to Denver. |
| 22 July 1983 | FAA clearance received for joint pilot type rating of 757/767. |
| 29 Sept 1983 | Japan Air Lines placed launch order for -300 with 6.4m fuselage stretch |
| 27 Mar 1984 | First 767ER commercial non-stop flight by El Al. |
| 1 June 1984 | Ethiopian 767 distance record of 6,524nm (12,082km) from DC to Addis Ababa. |
| 14 Jan 1986 | First 767-300 rolled out at Everett. |
| 25 Sept 1986 | First 767-300 delivered to Japan Air Lines. |

| | |
|---|---|
| 25 Mar 1987 | Rolls-Royce RB211-524H selected for 767. |
| 18 Apr 1988 | Mauritius 767 distance record of 7,582nm (14,042km) from Halifax in 16hr 27min. |
| 27 July 1989 | New distance record of 0000 miles (14,309km) from Grand Rapids to Seychelles. |
| 8 Feb 1990 | First Rolls-Royce powered 767 delivered to BA. |
| 10 June 1990 | New distance record of 7,726 miles (14,890km) from Seattle to Nairobi. |
| Nov 1991 | 400th 767 delivered. |
| Jan 1992 | 767AWACS announced |
| Oct 1992 | All Nippon Airways took delivery of their 30th 767. |
| 15 Jan 1993 | UPS launched the 767 Freighter with an order for 30 aircraft. |
| Nov 1993 | Japan ordered two E-767s |
| 20 May 1994 | 500th 767 completed and delivered to American Airlines in June. |
| Jan 1995 | Boeing announced 767 military tanker/transport. |
| 12 May 1995 | Roll-out of first 767 Freighter |
| 21 June 1995 | Maiden flight of first 767 Freighter. |
| 16 Oct 1995 | First delivery of 767 Freighter to UPS. |
| 9 Aug 1996 | Maiden flight of first E-767 for Japan. |
| 6 Jan 1997 | 767-ERX announced by Boeing. |
| March 1997 | Delta Air Lines placed launch order for 767-400ER. |
| 11 Mar 1998 | First two E-767s handed over to Japan at Boeing Field. |
| May 1998 | 700th 767 delivered. |

# 9 PRODUCTION LIST

| C/n | Series | Line No. | Operator | Identity | Fate |
|---|---|---|---|---|---|
| 21862 | 222 | 2 | United Airlines | N601UA | |
| 21863 | 222ER | 3 | United Airlines | N602UA | |
| 21864 | 222 | 4 | United Airlines | N603UA | |
| 21865 | 222 | 5 | United Airlines | N604UA | |
| 21866 | 222ER | 7 | United Airlines | N605UA | |
| 21867 | 222ER | 9 | United Airlines | N606UA | |
| 21868 | 222ER | 10 | United Airlines | N607UA | |
| 21869 | 222ER | 11 | United Airlines | N608UA | |
| 21870 | 222ER | 13 | United Airlines | N609UA | |
| 21871 | 222ER | 15 | United Airlines | N610UA | |
| 21872 | 222ER | 20 | United Airlines | N611UA | |
| 21873 | 222 | 41 | United Airlines | N612UA | |
| 21874 | 222 | 42 | United Airlines | N613UA | |
| 21875 | 222 | 43 | United Airlines | N614UA | |
| 21876 | 222 | 45 | United Airlines | N615UA | |
| 21877 | 222 | 46 | United Airlines | N617UA | |
| 21878 | 222 | 48 | United Airlines | N618UA | |
| 21879 | 222 | 49 | United Airlines | N619UA | |
| 21880 | 222 | 50 | United Airlines | N620UA | |
| 22213 | 232 | 6 | Delta Air Lines | N101DA | |
| 22214 | 232 | 12 | Delta Air Lines | N102DA | |
| 22215 | 232 | 17 | Delta Air Lines | N103DA | |
| 22216 | 232 | 26 | Delta Air Lines | N104DA | |
| 22217 | 232 | 27 | Delta Air Lines | N105DA | |
| 22218 | 232 | 31 | Delta Air Lines | N106DA | |
| 22219 | 232 | 37 | Delta Air Lines | N107DL | |
| 22220 | 232 | 38 | Delta Air Lines | N108DL | |
| 22221 | 232 | 53 | Delta Air Lines | N109DL | |
| 22222 | 232 | 56 | Delta Air Lines | N110DL | |
| 22223 | 232 | 74 | Delta Air Lines | N111DN | |
| 22224 | 232 | 76 | Delta Air Lines | N112DL | |
| 22225 | 232 | 77 | Delta Air Lines | N113DA | |
| 22226 | 232 | 78 | Delta Air Lines | N114DL | |
| 22227 | 232 | 83 | Delta Air Lines | N115DA | |
| 22233 | 200 | 1 | Boeing prototype | N767BA | |
| 22307 | 223 | 8 | American Airlines | N301AA | |
| 22308 | 223 | 19 | American Airlines | N302AA | |
| 22309 | 223 | 23 | American Airlines | N303AA | |
| 22310 | 223 | 25 | American Airlines | N304AA | |
| 22311 | 223 | 34 | American Airlines | N305AA | |
| 22312 | 223 | 44 | American Airlines | N306AA | |
| 22313 | 223 | 72 | American Airlines | N307AA | |
| 22314 | 223 | 73 | American Airlines | N308AA | |
| 22315 | 223 | 94 | American Airlines | N312AA | |
| 22316 | 223 | 95 | American Airlines | N313AA | |
| 22317 | 223ER | 109 | American Airlines | N315AA | |
| 22318 | 223ER | 111 | American Airlines | N316AA | |
| 22319 | 223ER | 112 | American Airlines | N317AA | |
| 22320 | 223ER | 128 | American Airlines | N319AA | |
| 22321 | 223ER | 130 | American Airlines | N320AA | |
| 22322 | 223ER | 139 | American Airlines | N321AA | |
| 22323 | 223ER | 140 | American Airlines | N322AA | |
| 22324 | 223ER | 146 | American Airlines | N323AA | |
| 22325 | 223ER | 147 | American Airlines | N324AA | |
| 22326 | 223ER | 157 | American Airlines | N325AA | |
| 22327 | 223ER | 159 | American Airlines | N327AA | |
| 22328 | 223ER | 160 | American Airlines | N328AA | |
| 22329 | 223ER | 164 | American Airlines | N329AA | |
| 22330 | 223ER | 166 | American Airlines | N330AA | |
| 22331 | 223ER | 168 | American Airlines | N332AA | |

| C/n | Series | Line No. | Operator | Identity | Fate |
|---|---|---|---|---|---|
| 22332 | 223ER | 169 | American Airlines | N334AA | |
| 22333 | 223ER | 194 | American Airlines | N335AA | |
| 22334 | 223ER | 195 | American Airlines | N336AA | |
| 22335 | 223ER | 196 | American Airlines | N338AA | |
| 22336 | 223ER | 198 | American Airlines | N339AA | |
| 22517 | 233ER | 16 | Air Canada | C-GAUB | |
| 22518 | 233 | 22 | Air Canada | C-GAUE | |
| 22519 | 233 | 40 | Air Canada | C-GAUH | |
| 22520 | 233 | 47 | Air Canada | C-GAUN | |
| 22521 | 233 | 66 | Air Canada | C-GAUP | |
| 22522 | 233 | 75 | Air Canada | C-GAUS | |
| 22523 | 233 | 87 | Air Canada | C-GAUU | |
| 22524 | 233 | 88 | Air Canada | C-GAUW | |
| 22525 | 233 | 91 | Air Canada | C-GAUY | |
| 22526 | 233 | 92 | Air Canada | C-GAVA | |
| 22527 | 233ER | 102 | Air Canada | C-GAVC | |
| 22528 | 233ER | 105 | Air Canada | C-GAVF | |
| 22564 | 231ER | 14 | TWA | N601TW | |
| 22565 | 231ER | 21 | TWA | N602TW | |
| 22566 | 231ER | 29 | TWA | N603TW | |
| 22567 | 231ER | 30 | TWA | N604TW | |
| 22568 | 231ER | 33 | TWA | N605TW | |
| 22569 | 231ER | 39 | TWA | N606TW | |
| 22570 | 231ER | 63 | TWA | N607TW | |
| 22571 | 231ER | 64 | TWA | N608TW | |
| 22572 | 231ER | 65 | TWA | N609TW | |
| 22573 | 231ER | 70 | TWA | N610TW | |
| 22681 | 209ER | 18 | Air Canada | C-FVNM | |
| 22682 | 209ER | 60 | Air Canada | C-FUCL | |
| 22683 | 275ER | 36 | Air Canada | C-GPWA | |
| 22684 | 275ER | 52 | Air Canada | C-GPWB | |
| 22692 | 277 | 24 | Ansett Australia | VH-RMD | |
| 22693 | 277 | 28 | Ansett Australia | VH-RME | |
| 22694 | 277 | 32 | Ansett Australia | VH-RMF | |
| 22695 | 277 | 35 | Ansett Australia | VH-RMG | |
| 22696 | 277 | 100 | Ansett Australia | VH-RMH | |
| 22785 | 281 | 51 | All Nippon Airways | JA8479 | Airborne Express, N767AX |
| 22786 | 281 | 54 | All Nippon Airways | JA8480 | Airborne Express, N768AX |
| 22787 | 281 | 58 | All Nippon Airways | JA8481 | Airborne Express, N769AX |
| 22788 | 281 | 61 | All Nippon Airways | JA8482 | Airborne Express, N773AX |
| 22789 | 281 | 67 | All Nippon Airways | JA8483 | Airborne Express, N774AX |
| 22790 | 281 | 69 | All Nippon Airways | JA8484 | Airborne Express, N775AX |
| 22921 | 2Q4 | 55 | Transbrasil | PT-TAA | |

Ready for departure from the flight line at Everett is LOT 767-35DER SP-LPA *Warsaw*, the first of three 767-300ERs for the airline. *Boeing*

| C/n | Series | Line No. | Operator | Identity | Fate |
|-----|--------|----------|----------|----------|------|
| 22922 | 2Q4 | 57 | Transbrasil | PT-TAB | |
| 22923 | 2Q4 | 59 | Transbrasil | PT-TAC | |
| 22972 | 258 | 62 | El Al | 4X-EAA | |
| 22973 | 258 | 68 | El Al | 4X EAB | |
| 22974 | 258ER | 86 | El Al | 4X-EAC | |
| 22975 | 258ER | 89 | El Al | 4X-EAD | |
| 22980 | 204 | 71 | Ansett Australia | VH-RML | lsd from Britannia G-BKPW |
| 22981 | 204 | 79 | Ansett Australia | VH-RMK | ex Britannia G-BKVZ |
| 23016 | 281 | 80 | All Nippon Airways | JA8485 | Airborne Express, N783AX |
| 23017 | 281 | 82 | All Nippon Airways | JA8486 | Airborne Express, N784AX |
| 23018 | 281 | 84 | All Nippon Airways | JA8487 | Airborne Express, N785AX |
| 23019 | 281 | 85 | All Nippon Airways | JA8488 | Airborne Express, N786AX |
| 23020 | 281 | 96 | All Nippon Airways | JA8489 | Airborne Express, N787AX |
| 23021 | 281 | 103 | All Nippon Airways | JA8490 | Airborne Express, N789AX |
| 23022 | 281 | 104 | All Nippon Airways | JA8491 | |
| 23057 | 205ER | 81 | TWA | N650TW | |
| 23058 | 205ER | 101 | TWA | N651TW | |
| 23072 | 204 | 107 | Air Europa | EC-GOJ | ex Air N Z ZK-NBI |
| 23106 | 260ER | 90 | Ethiopian Airlines | ET-AIE | |
| 23107 | 260ER | 93 | Ethiopian Airlines | ET-AIF | |
| 23140 | 281 | 106 | All Nippon Airways | JA8238 | |
| 23141 | 281 | 108 | All Nippon Airways | JA8239 | |
| 23142 | 281 | 110 | All Nippon Airways | JA8240 | |
| 23143 | 281 | 114 | All Nippon Airways | JA8241 | |
| 23144 | 281 | 115 | All Nippon Airways | JA8242 | |
| 23145 | 281 | 116 | All Nippon Airways | JA8243 | |
| 23146 | 281 | 121 | All Nippon Airways | JA8244 | |
| 23147 | 281 | 123 | All Nippon Airways | JA8245 | |
| 23178 | 266ER | 97 | Egyptair | SU-GAH | re-reg N767ER |
| 23179 | 266ER | 98 | Egyptair | SU-GAJ | SAA as ZS-SRB |
| 23180 | 266ER | 99 | Egyptair | SU-GAJ | SAA as ZS-SRC |
| 23212 | 246 | 117 | Japan Air Lines | JA8231 | |
| 23213 | 246 | 118 | Japan Air Lines | JA8232 | |
| 23214 | 246 | 122 | Japan Air Lines | JA8233 | |
| 23215 | 346 | 132 | Japan Air Lines | JA8236 | |
| 23216 | 346 | 148 | Japan Air Lines | JA8234 | |
| 23217 | 346 | 150 | Japan Air Lines | JA8235 | |
| 23250 | 204ER | 113 | Air New Zealand | ZK-NBJ | ex Britannia G-BLKW |
| 23275 | 332 | 136 | Delta Air Lines | N116DL | |
| 23276 | 332 | 151 | Delta Air Lines | N117DL | |
| 23277 | 332 | 152 | Delta Air Lines | N118DL | |
| 23278 | 332 | 153 | Delta Air Lines | N119DL | |
| 23279 | 332 | 154 | Delta Air Lines | N120DL | |
| 23280 | 269ER | 131 | Kuwait Airways | 9K-AIA | To ALAS as HI-660CA, Birgenair as TR-LEJ |
| 23281 | 269ER | 135 | Kuwait Airways | 9K-AIB | Written off Baghdad 2.91 |
| 23282 | 269ER | 138 | Kuwait Airways | 9K-AIC | Written off Baghdad 2.91 |
| 23304 | 238ER | 119 | Qantas | VH-EAJ | |
| 23305 | 238ER | 120 | Qantas | VH-EAK | |
| 23306 | 238ER | 125 | Qantas | VH-EAL | |
| 23307 | 2J6ER | 126 | Air China | B-2551 | |
| 23308 | 2J6ER | 127 | Air China | B-2552 | |
| 23309 | 238ER | 129 | Qantas | VH-EAM | |
| 23326 | 219ER | 124 | Air New Zealand | ZK-NBA | lsd to Ansett as VH-RMC |
| 23327 | 219ER | 134 | Air New Zealand | ZK-NBB | |
| 23328 | 219ER | 149 | Air New Zealand | ZK-NBC | |
| 23402 | 238ER | 133 | Qantas | VH-EAN | |
| 23403 | 238ER | 137 | Qantas | VH-EAO | |
| 23431 | 281 | 143 | All Nippon Airways | JA8251 | |
| 23432 | 281 | 145 | All Nippon Airways | JA8252 | |
| 23433 | 281 | 167 | All Nippon Airways | JA8254 | |
| 23434 | 281 | 171 | All Nippon Airways | JA8255 | |
| 23435 | 332 | 162 | Delta Air Lines | N121DE | |
| 23436 | 332 | 163 | Delta Air Lines | N122DL | |
| 23437 | 332 | 188 | Delta Air Lines | N123DN | |
| 23438 | 332 | 189 | Delta Air Lines | N124DE | |
| 23494 | 2S1 | 141 | TACA | N767TA | Written off Guatemala 5.4.93 |
| 23623 | 216ER | 142 | TACA | N762TA | |
| 23624 | 216ER | 144 | Transbrasil | PT-TAH | ex CC-CJV |
| 23645 | 346 | 174 | Japan Trans Ocean | JA8253 | |

| C/n | Series | Line No. | Operator | Identity | Fate |
|-----|--------|----------|----------|----------|------|
| 23744 | 2J6ER | 155 | Air China | B-2553 | |
| 23745 | 2J6ER | 156 | Air China | B-2554 | |
| 23756 | 381 | 176 | All Nippon Airways | JA8256 | |
| 23757 | 381 | 177 | All Nippon Airways | JA8257 | |
| 23758 | 381 | 179 | All Nippon Airways | JA8258 | |
| 23759 | 381 | 185 | All Nippon Airways | JA8259 | |
| 23764 | 3P6ER | 158 | Transbrasil | PT-TAL | |
| 23765 | 3Z9ER | 165 | Lauda Air | OE-LAU | |
| 23801 | 241ER | 170 | Varig | PP-VNO | |
| 23802 | 241ER | 172 | Varig | PP-VNP | |
| 23803 | 241ER | 161 | Varig | PP-VNN | |
| 23804 | 241ER | 178 | Varig | PP-VNQ | |
| 23805 | 241ER | 180 | Varig | PP-VNR | |
| 23806 | 241ER | 181 | Varig | PP-VNS | |
| 23807 | 204ER | 184 | Britannia Airways | G-BNCW | to Ansett as VH-RMO |
| 23896 | 238ER | 183 | Qantas | VH-EAQ | |
| 23897 | 201ER | 173 | US Airways | N645US | |
| 23898 | 201ER | 175 | US Airways | N646US | |
| 23899 | 201ER | 182 | US Airways | N647US | |
| 23900 | 201ER | 190 | US Airways | N648US | |
| 23901 | 201ER | 197 | US Airways | N649US | |
| 23902 | 201ER | 217 | US Airways | N650US | |
| 23916 | 260ER | 187 | Ethiopian Airlines | ET-AIZ | |
| 23961 | 346 | 192 | Japan Air Lines | JA8265 | |
| 23962 | 346 | 193 | Japan Trans Ocean | JA8267 | |
| 23963 | 346 | 224 | Japan Air Lines | JA8268 | |
| 23964 | 346 | 225 | Japan Air Lines | JA8269 | |
| 23965 | 346 | 186 | Japan Air Lines | JA8264 | |
| 23966 | 346 | 191 | Japan Asia Airways | JA8266 | |
| 23973 | 23BER | 208 | Air Mauritius | 3B-NAK | |
| 23974 | 23BER | 214 | Air Mauritius | 3B-NAL | |
| 24002 | 381 | 199 | All Nippon Airways | JA8271 | |
| 24003 | 381 | 212 | All Nippon Airways | JA8272 | |
| 24004 | 381 | 218 | All Nippon Airways | JA8273 | |
| 24005 | 381 | 222 | All Nippon Airways | JA8274 | |
| 24006 | 381 | 223 | All Nippon Airways | JA8275 | |
| 24007 | 2J6ER | 204 | Air China | B-2555 | |
| 24013 | 204ER | 210 | Britannia Airways | G-BNYS | |
| 24032 | 323ER | 202 | American Airlines | N351AA | |
| 24033 | 323ER | 205 | American Airlines | N352AA | |
| 24034 | 323ER | 206 | American Airlines | N353AA | |
| 24035 | 323ER | 211 | American Airlines | N354AA | |
| 24036 | 323ER | 221 | American Airlines | N355AA | |
| 24037 | 323ER | 226 | American Airlines | N39356 | |
| 24038 | 323ER | 227 | American Airlines | N357AA | |
| 24039 | 323ER | 228 | American Airlines | N358AA | |
| 24040 | 323ER | 230 | American Airlines | N359AA | |
| 24041 | 323ER | 232 | American Airlines | N360AA | |
| 24042 | 323ER | 235 | American Airlines | N361AA | |
| 24043 | 323ER | 237 | American Airlines | N362AA | |
| 24044 | 323ER | 238 | American Airlines | N363AA | |
| 24045 | 323ER | 240 | American Airlines | N39364 | |
| 24046 | 323ER | 241 | American Airlines | N39365 | |
| 24075 | 332 | 200 | Delta Air Lines | N125DL | |
| 24076 | 332 | 201 | Delta Air Lines | N126DL | |
| 24077 | 332 | 203 | Delta Air Lines | N127DL | |
| 24078 | 332 | 207 | Delta Air Lines | N128DL | |
| 24079 | 332 | 209 | Delta Air Lines | N129DL | |
| 24080 | 332 | 216 | Delta Air Lines | N130DL | |
| 24082 | 375ER | 213 | Canadian Airlines | C-FCAB | |
| 24083 | 375ER | 215 | Canadian Airlines | C-FCAE | |
| 24084 | 375ER | 219 | Canadian Airlines | C-FCAF | |
| 24085 | 375ER | 220 | Canadian Airlines | C-FCAG | |
| 24086 | 375ER | 248 | Canadian Airlines | C-FCAJ | to VARIG as PP-VPV |
| 24087 | 375ER | 249 | Canadian Airlines | C-FCAU | to VARIG as PP-VPW |
| 24142 | 233ER | 229 | Air Canada | C-GDSP | |
| 24143 | 233ER | 233 | Air Canada | C-GDSS | |
| 24144 | 233ER | 234 | Air Canada | C-GDSU | |
| 24145 | 233ER | 236 | Air Canada | C-GDSY | |

| C/n | Series | Line No. | Operator | Identity | Fate |
|-----|--------|----------|----------|----------|------|
| 24146 | 338ER | 231 | Qantas | VH-OGA | |
| 24150 | 219ER | 239 | Transbrasil | PT-TAG | ex ZK-NBE |
| 24157 | 2J6ER | 253 | Air China | B-2556 | |
| 24239 | 204ER | 243 | Britannia Airways | G-BOPB | |
| 24257 | 3G5ER | 251 | LTU-Sud | D-AMUR | |
| 24258 | 3G5ER | 255 | LTU-Sud | D-AMUS | |
| 24259 | 3G5ER | 268 | LTU-Sud | D-AMUN | |
| 24306 | 375ER | 258 | Canadian Airlines | C-FPCA | |
| 24307 | 375ER | 259 | Canadian Airlines | C-FTCA | |
| 24316 | 338ER | 242 | Qantas | VH-OGB | |
| 24317 | 338ER | 246 | Qantas | VH-OGC | |
| 24318 | 383ER | 257 | SAS | SE-DKO | LN-RCH |
| 24323 | 233ER | 250 | Air Canada | C-FBEF | |
| 24324 | 233ER | 252 | Air Canada | C-FBEG | |
| 24325 | 233ER | 254 | Air Canada | C-FBEM | |
| 24333 | 336ER | 265 | British Airways | G-BNWA | |
| 24334 | 336ER | 281 | British Airways | G-BNWB | |
| 24335 | 336ER | 284 | British Airways | G-BNWC | |
| 24336 | 336ER | 286 | British Airways | G-BNWD | |
| 24337 | 336ER | 288 | British Airways | G-BNWE | |
| 24338 | 336ER | 293 | British Airways | G-BNWF | |
| 24339 | 336ER | 298 | British Airways | G-BNWG | |
| 24340 | 336ER | 335 | British Airways | G-BNWH | *Waves of the City* |
| 24341 | 336ER | 342 | British Airways | G-BNWI | |
| 24342 | 336ER | 363 | British Airways | G-BNWJ | |
| 24343 | 336ER | 364 | British Airways | G-BNWK | |
| 24349 | 3P6ER | 244 | Transbrasil | PT-TAM | ex A40-GG Gulf Air |
| 24350 | 381 | 245 | All Nippon Airways | JA8285 | |
| 24351 | 381 | 271 | All Nippon Airways | JA8287 | |
| 24357 | 383ER | 262 | Avianca | N984AN | ex LN-RCB |
| 24358 | 383ER | 263 | SAS | OY-KDH | |
| 24400 | 381ER | 269 | All Nippon Airways | JA8286 | |
| 24407 | 338ER | 247 | Qantas | VH-OGD | |
| 24415 | 381 | 276 | All Nippon Airways | JA8288 | |
| 24416 | 381 | 280 | All Nippon Airways | JA8289 | |
| 24417 | 381 | 290 | All Nippon Airways | JA8290 | |
| 24428 | 31AER | 279 | Martinair | PH-MCG | |

| C/n | Series | Line No. | Operator | Identity | Fate |
|---|---|---|---|---|---|
| 24429 | 31AER | 294 | Martinair | PH-MCH | |
| 24448 | 2Q8ER | 272 | Air Seychelles | S7-AAS | |
| 24457 | 204ER | 256 | Air Europa | EC-GHM | |
| 24475 | 383ER | 273 | SAS | OY-KDI | LN-RCG |
| 24476 | 383ER | 274 | SAS | SE-DOB | LN-RCI |
| 24477 | 383ER | 337 | SAS | OY-KDL | |
| 24484 | 3P6ER | 260 | Gulf Air | A40-GH | |
| 24485 | 3P6ER | 264 | Gulf Air | A40-GI | |
| 24495 | 3P6ER | 267 | Gulf Air | A40-GJ | |
| 24496 | 3P6ER | 270 | Gulf Air | A40-GK | |
| 24498 | 346 | 277 | Japan Air Lines | JA8299 | |
| 24531 | 338ER | 278 | Qantas | VH-OGE | |
| 24541 | 366ER | 275 | Egyptair | SU-GAO | |
| 24542 | 366ER | 282 | Egyptair | SU-GAP | |
| 24574 | 375ER | 302 | Canadian Airlines | C-FXCA | |
| 24575 | 375ER | 311 | Canadian Airlines | C-FOCA | |
| 24618 | 259ER | 292 | Avianca | N985AN | |
| 24628 | 3Z9ER | 283 | Lauda Air | OE-LAV | w/o 26.5.91 over Thailand |
| 24632 | 381ER | 285 | All Nippon Airways | JA8362 | |
| 24713 | 2N0ER | 287 | Air Zimbabwe | Z-WPE | |
| 24716 | 284ER | 297 | LAN-Chile | CC-CDH | |
| 24727 | 283ER | 301 | Transbrasil | PT-TAI | ex SE-DKP |
| 24728 | 283ER | 305 | Transbrasil | PT-TAJ | ex LN-RCC |
| 24729 | 383ER | 358 | SAS | SE-DKU | LN-RCK |
| 24733 | 25DER | 261 | LOT Polish Airlines | SP-LOA | |
| 24734 | 25DER | 266 | LOT Polish Airlines | SP-LOB | |
| 24736 | 204ER | 296 | Britannia Airways | G-BRIF | |
| 24742 | 284ER | 303 | Avianca | N988AN | VH-RMA, ex V8-RBD |
| 24745 | 3Q8ER | 355 | Air France | F-GHGF | |
| 24746 | 3Q8ER | 378 | Air France | G-GHGG | |
| 24752 | 341 | 289 | VARIG | PP-VOI | |
| 24753 | 341ER | 291 | VARIG | PP-VOJ | |
| 24755 | 381 | 295 | All Nippon Airways | JA8291 | |
| 24756 | 381 | 300 | All Nippon Airways | JA8363 | |
| 24757 | 204ER | 299 | Britannia Airways | G-BRIG | |
| 24759 | 332ER | 304 | Delta Air Lines | N171DN | |
| 24762 | 284ER | 307 | LAN-Chile | CC-CDJ | |
| 24764 | 2B7ER | 306 | US Airways | N651US | |
| 24765 | 2B7ER | 308 | US Airways | N652US | |
| 24766 | 3D6ER | 310 | Air Algerie | 7T-VJG | |
| 24767 | 3D6ER | 323 | Air Algerie | 7T-VJH | |
| 24768 | 3D6ER | 332 | Air Algerie | 7T-VJI | |
| 24775 | 332ER | 312 | Delta Air Lines | N172DN | |
| 24782 | 346 | 327 | Japan Air Lines | JA8364 | |
| 24783 | 346 | 329 | Japan Air Lines | JA8365 | |
| 24797 | 38EER | 328 | Asiana | HL7263 | |
| 24798 | 38EER | 331 | Asiana | HL7264 | |
| 24800 | 332ER | 313 | Delta Air Lines | N173DN | |
| 24802 | 332ER | 317 | Delta Air Lines | N174DN | |
| 24803 | 332ER | 318 | Delta Air Lines | N175DN | |
| 24832 | 27AER | 316 | Balkan Bulgarian A/L | F-GHGD | leased from Air France |
| 24835 | 259ER | 321 | Avianca | N986AN | |
| 24843 | 341ER | 314 | VARIG | PP-VOK | |
| 24844 | 341ER | 324 | VARIG | PP-VOL | |
| 24846 | 383ER | 309 | SAS | SE-DKR | LN-RCE |
| 24847 | 383ER | 315 | SAS | LN-RCD | |
| 24848 | 383ER | 325 | SAS | SE-DKS | OY-KDN |
| 24849 | 383ER | 330 | SAS | SE-DKT | OY-KDO |
| 24852 | 332 | 320 | Delta Air Lines | N131DN | |
| 24853 | 338ER | 319 | Qantas | VH-OGF | |
| 24854 | 27AER | 326 | Balkan Bulgarian A/L | F-GHGE | leased from Air France |
| 24865 | 35DER | 322 | LOT-Polish Airlines | SP-LPA | |
| 24867 | 25DER | 333 | Air Zimbabwe | Z-WPF | |
| 24875 | 219ER | 371 | Air New Zealand | ZK-NCE | |
| 24876 | 219ER | 413 | Air New Zealand | ZK-NCF | |
| 24880 | 381 | 336 | All Nippon Airways | JA8368 | |

LEFT: New BA 767-336ER G-BZHA, the first of three ordered in June 1997, is prepared for the production test flight at Everett in May 1998, and features the new colours. This was the 702nd 767 off the line. *Philip Birtles*

| C/n | Series | Line No. | Operator | Identity | Fate |
|-----|--------|----------|----------|----------|------|
| 24894 | 2B7ER | 338 | US Airways | N653US | |
| 24929 | 338ER | 343 | Qantas | VH-OGG | |
| 24930 | 338ER | 344 | Qantas | VH-OGH | |
| 24947 | 3Y0ER | 351 | LAN-Chile | CC-CEY | |
| 24948 | 3Y0ER | 380 | Transbrasil | PT-TAE | |
| 24953 | 3Y0ER | 405 | TWA | N632TW | |
| 24973 | 216ER | 347 | Ansett | VH-RMM | |
| 24981 | 332 | 345 | Delta Airlines | N132DN | |
| 24982 | 332 | 348 | Delta Airlines | N133DN | |
| 24983 | 3P6ER | 334 | Gulf Air | A40-GL | to Delta as N1501P |
| 24984 | 3P6ER | 339 | Gulf Air | A40-GM | to Delta as N152DL |
| 24985 | 3P6ER | 340 | Gulf Air | A40-GN | to Delta as N153DL |
| 24999 | 3Y0ER | 354 | Spanair | EC-FCU | |
| 25000 | 3Y0ER | 386 | Spanair | EC-FHA | |
| 25055 | 381 | 352 | All Nippon Airways | JA8360 | |
| 25058 | 204ER | 362 | Britannia Airways | G-BYAA | |
| 25061 | 332ER | 341 | Delta Air Lines | N176DN | |
| 25076 | 3T7ER | 366 | Eva Airways | B-16601 | |
| 25077 | 37EER | 385 | Air France | F-GHGH | |
| 25088 | 383ER | 359 | SAS | OY-KDM | |
| 25091 | 322ER | 360 | United Airlines | N641UA | |
| 25092 | 322ER | 367 | United Airlines | N642UA | |
| 25093 | 322ER | 368 | United Airlines | N643UA | |
| 25094 | 322ER | 369 | United Airlines | N644UA | |
| 25117 | 3T7ER | 370 | Eva Airways | B-16602 | N602EV |
| 25120 | 375ER | 361 | Canadian Airlines | C-GLCA | |
| 25121 | 375ER | 372 | Canadian Airlines | C-GSCA | ex China Southern B-2546 |
| 25122 | 332ER | 346 | Delta Air Lines | N177DN | |
| 25123 | 332 | 353 | Delta Air Lines | N134DL | |
| 25132 | 38EER | 417 | Asiana | HL7268 | |
| 25136 | 381ER | 379 | All Nippon Airways | JA8356 | |
| 25137 | 330ER | 377 | TWA | N691LF | ex D-ABUX |
| 25139 | 204ER | 373 | Britannia Airways | G-BYAB | |
| 25143 | 332ER | 349 | Delta Air Lines | N178DN | |
| 25144 | 332ER | 350 | Delta Air Lines | N179DN | |
| 25145 | 332 | 356 | Delta Air Lines | N135DL | |
| 25146 | 332 | 374 | Delta Air Lines | N136DL | |
| 25170 | 31BER | 542 | China Southern | B-2566 | |
| 25193 | 323ER | 388 | American Airlines | N366AA | |
| 25194 | 323ER | 394 | American Airlines | N39367 | |
| 25195 | 323ER | 404 | American Airlines | N368AA | |
| 25196 | 323ER | 422 | American Airlines | N369AA | |
| 25197 | 323ER | 430 | American Airlines | N370AA | |
| 25198 | 323ER | 431 | American Airlines | N371AA | |
| 25199 | 323ER | 433 | American Airlines | N372AA | |
| 25200 | 323ER | 435 | American Airlines | N373AA | |
| 25201 | 323ER | 437 | American Airlines | N374AA | |
| 25202 | 323ER | 441 | American Airlines | N7375A | |
| 25203 | 336ER | 365 | British Airways | G-BNWL | |
| 25204 | 336ER | 376 | British Airways | G-BNWM | |
| 25208 | 330ER | 381 | Air Europe Italy | EI-CIY | ex D-ABUY |
| 25209 | 330ER | 382 | Condor | D-ABUZ | ex TWA N634TW |
| 25221 | 3S1ER | 384 | Britannia Airways | G-BXOP | ex EVA B-16688 |
| 25225 | 2B7ER | 375 | US Airways | N654US | |
| 25241 | 3P6ER | 389 | Gulf Air | A40-GO | to Delta as N154DL |
| 25246 | 338ER | 387 | Qantas | VH-OGI | |
| 25257 | 2B7ER | 383 | US Airways | N655US | |
| 25269 | 3P6ER | 390 | Gulf Air | A40-GP | to Delta as N155DL |
| 25273 | 31AER | 393 | Lauda Air | OE-LAT | |
| 25274 | 338ER | 396 | Qantas | VH-OGJ | |
| 25280 | 322ER | 391 | United Airlines | N645UA | |
| 25283 | 322ER | 420 | United Airlines | N646UA | |
| 25284 | 322ER | 424 | United Airlines | N647UA | |
| 25285 | 322ER | 443 | United Airlines | N648UA | |
| 25286 | 322ER | 444 | United Airlines | N649UA | |
| 25287 | 322ER | 449 | United Airlines | N650UA | |
| 25293 | 381 | 401 | All Nippon Airways | JA8357 | |
| 25306 | 332 | 392 | Delta Air Lines | N137DL | |
| 25312 | 31AER | 400 | Martinair | PH-MCI | |

| C/n | Series | Line No. | Operator | Identity | Fate |
|---|---|---|---|---|---|
| 25316 | 338ER | 397 | Qantas | VH-OGK | |
| 25346 | 33AER | 403 | Royal Brunei | V8-RBE | |
| 25347 | 38EER | 399 | Asiana | HL7266 | |
| 25354 | 3P6ER | 406 | Gulf Air | A40-GR | to Delta as N156DL |
| 25363 | 338ER | 402 | Qantas | VH-OGL | |
| 25365 | 383ER | 395 | SAS | SE-DKX | LN-RCL |
| 25389 | 322ER | 452 | United Airlines | N651UA | |
| 25390 | 322ER | 457 | United Airlines | N652UA | |
| 25391 | 322ER | 460 | United Airlines | N653UA | |
| 25392 | 322ER | 462 | United Airlines | N654UA | |
| 25393 | 322ER | 468 | United Airlines | N655UA | |
| 25394 | 322ER | 472 | United Airlines | N656UA | |
| 25403 | 33AER | 409 | LAN-Chile | CC-CEU | |
| 25404 | 38EER | 411 | Asiana | HL7267 | |
| 25409 | 332 | 410 | Delta Air Lines | N138DL | |
| 25411 | 3Y0ER | 408 | Air Europe Italy | EI-CLR | to Aeromexico as XA-TJD |
| 25421 | 2B1ER | 407 | Transbrasil | PT-TAK | |
| 25442 | 336ER | 418 | British Airways | G-BNWO | |
| 25443 | 336ER | 419 | British Airways | G-BNWP | |
| 25444 | 336ER | 398 | British Airways | G-BNWN | |
| 25445 | 323ER | 447 | American Airlines | N376AN | |
| 25446 | 323ER | 453 | American Airlines | N377AN | |
| 25447 | 323ER | 469 | American Airlines | N378AN | |
| 25448 | 323ER | 481 | American Airlines | N379AA | |
| 25449 | 323ER | 489 | American Airlines | N380AN | |
| 25450 | 323ER | 495 | American Airlines | N381AN | |
| 25451 | 323ER | 498 | American Airlines | N382AN | |
| 25530 | 33AER | 414 | Royal Brunei | V8-RBF | |
| 25531 | 33AER | 423 | LTU-Sud | D-AMUP | |
| 25532 | 33AER | 442 | Royal Brunei | V8-RBG | |
| 25533 | 33AER | 454 | Royal Brunei | V8-RBJ | |
| 25534 | 33AER | 477 | Royal Brunei | V8-RBH | |
| 25535 | 33AER | 491 | Vietnam Airlines | VH-NOE | to Challeng Air as OO-VAS, lsd to Air Namibia |
| 25536 | 33AER | 504 | Royal Brunei | V8-RBK | |
| 25537 | 27GER | 517 | Government of Brunei | V8-MJB | |
| 25575 | 338ER | 451 | Qantas | VH-OGM | |
| 25576 | 338ER | 549 | Qantas | VH-OGN | |
| 25577 | 338ER | 550 | Qantas | VH-OGO | |
| 25583 | 333ER | 508 | Air Canada | C-FMWP | |
| 25584 | 333ER | 596 | Air Canada | C-FMWQ | |
| 25585 | 333ER | 597 | Air Canada | C-FMWU | |
| 25586 | 333ER | 599 | Air Canada | C-FMWV | |
| 25587 | 333ER | 604 | Air Canada | C-FMWY | |
| 25588 | 333ER | 606 | Air Canada | C-FMXC | |
| 25616 | 381ER | 432 | All Nippon Airways | JA8358 | |
| 25617 | 381ER | 439 | All Nippon Airways | JA8359 | |
| 25618 | 381 | 458 | All Nippon Airways | JA8322 | |
| 25619 | 381ER | 645 | All Nippon Airways | JA8970 | |
| 25654 | 381ER | 463 | All Nippon Airways | JA8323 | |
| 25655 | 381 | 465 | All Nippon Airways | JA8324 | |
| 25656 | 381 | 510 | All Nippon Airways | JA8567 | |
| 25657 | 381 | 515 | All Nippon Airways | JA8568 | |
| 25658 | 381 | 519 | All Nippon Airways | JA8578 | |
| 25659 | 381 | 520 | All Nippon Airways | JA8579 | |
| 25660 | 381 | 539 | All Nippon Airways | JA8670 | |
| 25661 | 381 | 543 | All Nippon Airways | JA8674 | |
| 25662 | 381 | 551 | All Nippon Airways | JA8677 | |
| 25732 | 336ER | 421 | British Airways | G-BNWR | |
| 25733 | 336ER | 648 | British Airways | G-BNWZ | |
| 25757 | 38EER | 523 | Asiana | HL7247 | |
| 25758 | 38E | 582 | Asiana | HL7248 | |
| 25760 | 38E | 639 | Asiana | HL7506 | |
| 25761 | 38EFER | 616 | Asiana | HL7507 | |
| 25762 | 38E | 658 | Asiana | HL7515 | |
| 25763 | 38E | 656 | Asiana | HL7514 | |
| 25826 | 336ER | 473 | British Airways | G-BNWS | |
| 25828 | 336ER | 476 | British Airways | G-BNWT | |
| 25829 | 336ER | 483 | British Airways | G-BNWU | |

| C/n | Series | Line No. | Operator | Identity | Fate |
|---|---|---|---|---|---|
| 25831 | 336ER | 526 | British Airways | G-BNWW | |
| 25832 | 336ER | 529 | British Airways | G-BNWX | |
| 25834 | 336ER | 608 | British Airways | G-BNWY | |
| 25864 | 375ER | 426 | LAN Chile | CC-CRH | ex China Southern B-2562 |
| 25865 | 375ER | 430 | LAN Chile | CC-CRG | ex China Southern B-2561 |
| 25875 | 3J6ER | 429 | Air China | B-2557 | |
| 25876 | 3J6ER | 478 | Air China | B-2558 | |
| 25877 | 3J6ER | 530 | Air China | B-2559 | |
| 25878 | 3J6ER | 569 | Air China | B-2560 | |
| 25984 | 332 | 427 | Delta Air Lines | N139DL | |
| 25985 | 332ER | 428 | Delta Air Lines | N180DN | |
| 25986 | 332ER | 446 | Delta Air Lines | N181DN | |
| 25987 | 332ER | 461 | Delta Air Lines | N182DN | |
| 25988 | 332 | 499 | Delta Air Lines | N140LL | |
| 25989 | 332 | 506 | Delta Air Lines | N1402A | |
| 25990 | 332ER | 646 | Delta Air Lines | N189DN | |
| 25991 | 332 | 721 | Delta Air Lines | N143DA | |
| 26063 | 35EER | 434 | EVA Airways | B-16603 | |
| 26064 | 35EER | 438 | EVA Airways | B-16605 | |
| 26200 | 3Y0ER | 450 | Aero Mexico | XA-RKI | |
| 26204 | 3Y0ER | 464 | Lan Chile | CC-CEL | ex Aero Mexico XA-RKJ |
| 26205 | 3Y0ER | 474 | Aeroflot | EI-CKD | |
| 26206 | 3Y0ER | 487 | Iberia | EC-GSU | ex Asiana HL7269 |
| 26207 | 3Y0ER | 503 | Iberia | EC- | ex Asiana HL7286 |
| 26208 | 3Y0ER | 505 | Aeroflot | EI-CKE | |
| 26233 | 3P6ER | 501 | Gulf Air | A40-GU | |
| 26234 | 3P6ER | 538 | Gulf Air | A40-GY | |
| 26235 | 3P6ER | 502 | Gulf Air | A40-GV | |
| 26236 | 3P6ER | 436 | Gulf Air | A40-GS | |
| 26237 | 3P6ER | 544 | Gulf Air | A40-GZ | |
| 26238 | 3P6ER | 440 | Gulf Air | A40-GT | |
| 26256 | 39HER | 484 | Leisure International | G-UKLH | |
| 26257 | 39HER | 488 | Leisure International | G-UKLI | |
| 26259 | 31BER | 534 | China Southern | B-2565 | |
| 26260 | 3X2ER | 552 | Air Pacific | DQ-FJC | |
| 26261 | 3Q8ER | 575 | LAN-Chile | CC-CDM | |
| 26262 | 352ER | 583 | Air Europe Italy | EI-CLS | |
| 26263 | 306ER | 592 | KLM | PH-BZC | |
| 26264 | 319ER | 555 | Air New Zealand | ZK-NCH | |
| 26265 | 3B1ER | 570 | Asiana | HL7249 | |
| 26328 | 3Q8ER | 637 | Air Seychelles | S7-AHM | |
| 26387 | 35HER | 445 | Air Europe Italy | EI-CJA | ex S7-AAQ |
| 26388 | 35HER | 456 | Air Europe Italy | EI-CJB | ex S7-AAV |
| 26389 | 35HER | 459 | Air New Zealand | ZK-NCM | |
| 26417 | 3Z9ER | 448 | Lauda Air | OE-LAW | |
| 26469 | 31AER | 415 | Martinair | PH-MCL | |
| 26470 | 31AER | 416 | Martinair | PH-MCM | |
| 26471 | 2B1ER | 511 | SAA | ZS-SRA | |
| 26544 | 383ER | 412 | SAS | SE-DOC | |
| 26608 | 3S1ER | 559 | TACA | N769TA | |
| 26847 | 2B7ER | 486 | US Airways | N656US | |
| 26912 | 319ER | 509 | Air New Zealand | ZK-NCG | |
| 26913 | 319ER | 558 | Air New Zealand | ZK-NCI | |
| 26915 | 319ER | 574 | Air New Zealand | ZK-NCJ | |
| 26971 | 319ER | 663 | Air New Zealand | ZK-NCK | |
| 26983 | 330ER | 471 | Condor | D-ABUD | |
| 26984 | 330ER | 518 | Condor | D-ABUE | |
| 26985 | 330ER | 537 | Condor | D-ABUF | |
| 26986 | 330ER | 553 | Condor | D-ABUH | |
| 26987 | 330ER | 466 | Condor | D-ABUB | |
| 26988 | 330ER | 562 | Condor | D-ABUI | |
| 26991 | 330ER | 455 | Condor | D-ABUA | |
| 26992 | 330ER | 470 | Condor | D-ABUC | |
| 26995 | 323ER | 500 | American Airlines | N383AN | |
| 26996 | 323ER | 512 | American Airlines | N384AA | |
| 27048 | 27GER | 475 | Malev | HA-LHA | |
| 27049 | 27GER | 482 | Malev | HA-LHB | |
| 27050 | 381 | 516 | All Nippon Airways | JA8569 | |

| C/n | Series | Line No. | Operator | Identity | Fate |
|---|---|---|---|---|---|
| 27059 | 323ER | 536 | American Airlines | N385AM | |
| 27060 | 323ER | 540 | American Airlines | N386AA | |
| 27095 | 3Z9ER | 467 | Lauda Air | OE-LAX | |
| 27110 | 332ER | 492 | Delta Air Lines | N183DN | |
| 27111 | 332ER | 496 | Delta Air Lines | N184DN | |
| 27112 | 322ER | 479 | United Airlines | N657UA | |
| 27113 | 322ER | 480 | United Airlines | N658UA | |
| 27114 | 322ER | 485 | United Airlines | N659UA | |
| 27115 | 322ER | 494 | United Airlines | N660UA | |
| 27135 | 328ER | 493 | Air France | F-GHGI | |
| 27136 | 328ER | 497 | Air France | F-GHGJ | |
| 27140 | 336ER | 490 | British Airways | G-BNWV | |
| 27158 | 322ER | 507 | United Airlines | N661UA | |
| 27159 | 322ER | 513 | United Airlines | N662UA | |
| 27160 | 322ER | 514 | United Airlines | N663UA | |
| 27184 | 323ER | 541 | American Airlines | N387AM | |
| 27189 | 33AER | 521 | Royal Brunei | V8-RBL | |
| 27192 | 25E | 524 | EVA Airways | B-16621 | |
| 27193 | 25E | 527 | EVA Airways | B-16622 | |
| 27194 | 25E | 532 | EVA Airways | B-16623 | |
| 27195 | 25E | 535 | EVA Airways | B-16625 | |
| 27205 | 31KER | 528 | Airtours | G-SJMC | |
| 27206 | 31KER | 533 | Airtours | G-DAJC | |
| 27212 | 328ER | 531 | Sobelair | OO-STF | |
| 27239 | 34AFER | 580 | UPS | N301UP | |
| 27240 | 34AFER | 590 | UPS | N302UP | |
| 27241 | 34AFER | 594 | UPS | N303UP | |
| 27242 | 34AFER | 598 | UPS | N304UP | |
| 27243 | 34AFER | 600 | UPS | N305UP | |
| 27254 | 3P6ER | 522 | Gulf Air | A40-GW | re-reg VP-BKS by Kalair |
| 27255 | 3P6ER | 525 | Gulf Air | A40-GX | |
| 27309 | 36DER | 546 | Shanghai Airlines | B-2563 | |
| 27310 | 33AER | 545 | Sobelair | OO-SBY | |
| 27311 | 346 | 547 | Japan Air Lines | JA8397 | |
| 27312 | 346 | 548 | Japan Air Lines | JA8398 | |
| 27313 | 346 | 554 | Japan Air Lines | JA8399 | |
| 27339 | 381ER | 556 | All Nippon Airways | JA8664 | |
| 27376 | 33AER | 560 | Alitalia | I-DEIB | ex G-OITA |
| 27377 | 33AER | 561 | Alitalia | I-DEIC | ex G-OITB |
| 27385 | 27CER | 557 | Japanese Government | N767JA | AWACS 74-3501 |
| 27391 | 27CER | 588 | Japanese Government | N767JB | AWACS 74-3502 |
| 27392 | 324ER | 568 | Vietnam Airlines | S7-RGV | |
| 27393 | 324ER | 571 | Vietnam Airlines | S7-RGW | |
| 27394 | 324ER | 572 | Asiana | HL7505 | lsd to Delta as N394DL |
| 27427 | 328ER | 579 | Royal Brunei | V8-RBN | to Japan Pacific Airlines |
| 27428 | 328ER | 586 | Royal Brunei | V8-RBM | to Japan Pacific Airlines |
| 27429 | 328ER | | Air France | F-GIYQ | |
| 27444 | 381 | 567 | All Nippon Airways | JA8669 | |
| 27445 | 381 | 573 | All Nippon Airways | JA8342 | |
| 27448 | 323ER | 563 | American Airlines | N388AA | |
| 27449 | 323ER | 564 | American Airlines | N389AA | |
| 27450 | 323ER | 565 | American Airlines | N390AA | |
| 27451 | 323ER | 566 | American Airlines | N391AA | |
| 27468 | 33AER | 584 | Alitalia | I-DEID | ex G-OITC |
| 27476 | 33AER | 687 | Hokkaido Airlines | JA98AD | |
| 27568 | 324ER | 593 | Vietnam Airlines | S7-RGU | |
| 27569 | 324ER | 601 | Ansett Australia | VH-BZF | |
| 27582 | 332ER | 617 | Delta Air Lines | N187DN | |
| 27583 | 332ER | 631 | Delta Air Lines | N188DN | |
| 27584 | 332 | | Delta Air Lines | N144DA | |
| 27597 | 316ER | 602 | LAN Chile | CC-CDP | |
| 27600 | 3Q8ER | 655 | Air Europe Italy | EI-CNS | |
| 27610 | 306ER | 605 | KLM | PH-BZD | 8,000th Boeing Jet Airliner |
| 27611 | 306ER | 633 | KLM | PH-BZH | |
| 27612 | 306ER | 647 | KLM | PH-BZI | |
| 27613 | 316ER | 652 | LAN Chile | CC-CBJ | |
| 27614 | 306ER | 661 | KLM | PH-BZK | |
| 27615 | 316ER | 681 | LAN Chile | CC-CRT | |

| C/n | Series | Line No. | Operator | Identity | Fate |
|---|---|---|---|---|---|
| 27619 | 31AER | 595 | Martinair | PH-MCV | |
| 27658 | 346 | 581 | Japan Air Lines | JA8975 | |
| 27659 | 346 | 667 | Japan Asia Airways | JA8976 | |
| 27683 | 36DER | 686 | Shanghai Airlines | B-2567 | |
| 27740 | 34AFER | 628 | UPS | N309UP | |
| 27741 | 34AFER | 632 | UPS | N311UP | |
| 27742 | 34AFER | 638 | UPS | N314UP | |
| 27743 | 34AFER | 640 | UPS | N315UP | |
| 27744 | 34AFER | 660 | UPS | N316UP | |
| 27745 | 34AFER | 666 | UPS | N317UP | |
| 27746 | 34AFER | 670 | UPS | N318UP | |
| 27747 | 34AFER | 674 | UPS | N320UP | |
| 27748 | 34AFER | 678 | UPS | N322UP | |
| 27749 | 34AFER | 682 | UPS | N323UP | |
| 27758 | 34AFER | 672 | UPS | N319UP | |
| 27759 | 34AFER | 622 | UPS | N306UP | |
| 27760 | 34AFER | 624 | UPS | N307UP | |
| 27761 | 34AFER | 626 | UPS | N308UP | |
| 27762 | 34AFER | 630 | UPS | N310UP | |
| 27763 | 34AFER | 634 | UPS | N312UP | |
| 27764 | 34AFER | 636 | UPS | N313UP | |
| 27824 | 338ER | 662 | Qantas | VH-OGR | |
| 27825 | 338ER | 665 | Qantas | VH-OGS | |
| 27902 | 35DER | 577 | LOT Polish Airlines | SP-LPB | |
| 27908 | 33AER | 578 | Alitalia | I-DEIF | ex G-OITF |
| 27909 | 33AER | 591 | Lauda Air | OE-LAS | |
| 27918 | 33AER | 603 | Alitalia | I-DEIG | ex G-OITG |
| 27942 | 381ER | 651 | All Nippon Airways | JA8971 | |
| 27943 | 381 | 669 | All Nippon Airways | JA601A | |
| 27944 | 381 | 684 | All Nippon Airways | JA602A | |
| 27957 | 306ER | 587 | KLM | PH-BZA | |
| 27958 | 306ER | 589 | KLM | PH-BZB | |
| 27959 | 306ER | 609 | KLM | PH-BZF | |
| 27960 | 306ER | 625 | KLM | PH-BZG | |
| 27961 | 332ER | 576 | Delta Air Lines | N185DN | |
| 27962 | 332ER | 585 | Delta Air Lines | N186DN | |
| 27993 | 3Q8ER | 619 | Air Europe Italy | EI-CMQ | |
| 28016 | 27CER | 618 | Japanese Government | N767JC | AWACS 74-3503 |
| 28017 | 27CER | 642 | Japanese Government | N767JD | AWACS 74-3504 |
| 28028 | 304ER | 705 | Britannia Airways | D-AGYF | ex G-OBYF |
| 28039 | 304ER | 610 | Britannia Airways | G-OBYA | to D-AGYA |
| 28040 | 304ER | 613 | Britannia Airways | G-OBYB | |
| 28041 | 304ER | 614 | Britannia Airways | G-OBYC | to D-AGYC |
| 28042 | 304ER | 649 | Britannia Airways | G-OBYD | |
| 28098 | 306ER | 607 | KLM | PH-BZE | |
| 28111 | 3G5ER | 612 | LTU | D-AMUJ | |
| 28132 | 3Q8ER | 692 | TWA | N634TW | |
| 28147 | 33AER | 611 | Alitalia | I-DEIL | ex G-OITL |
| 28148 | 3W0ER | 620 | China Yunnan | B-2568 | |
| 28149 | 3W0ER | 627 | China Yunnan | B-2569 | |
| 28153 | 338ER | 615 | Qantas | VH-OGP | |
| 28154 | 338ER | 623 | Qantas | VH-OGQ | |
| 28159 | 33AER | 689 | City Bird | OO-CTQ | |
| 28206 | 3Q8ER | 694 | Transaero | N601LF | |
| 28207 | 3Q8ER | 714 | TWA | N635TW | |
| 28208 | 304ER | | Britannia Airways | G-OBYF | to D-AGYF |
| 28264 | 3W0ER | 644 | China Yunnan | B-5001 | |
| 28327 | 316ER | 621 | LAN Chile | CC-CEB | |
| 28329 | 316ER | 641 | LAN Chile | CC-CEK | |
| 28370 | 33PER | 635 | Uzbekistan Airways | UK-76701 | VP-BUA |
| 28392 | 33PER | 650 | Uzbekistan Airways | UK-76702 | VP-BUZ |
| 28447 | 332ER | 653 | Delta Air Lines | N190DN | |
| 28448 | 332ER | 654 | Delta Air Lines | N191DN | |
| 28449 | 332ER | 664 | Delta Air Lines | N192DN | |
| 28450 | 332ER | 671 | Delta Air Lines | N193DN | |
| 28451 | 332ER | 675 | Delta Air Lines | N194DN | |
| 28452 | 332ER | 676 | Delta Air Lines | N195DN | |
| 28453 | 332ER | 679 | Delta Air Lines | N196DN | |

| C/n | Series | Line No. | Operator | Identity | Fate |
|-----|--------|----------|----------|----------|------|
| 28454 | 332ER | 683 | Delta Air Lines | N197DN | |
| 28455 | 332ER | 685 | Delta Air Lines | N198DN | |
| 28456 | 332ER | 690 | Delta Air Lines | N199DN | |
| 28457 | 332ER | 696 | Delta Air Lines | N1200K | |
| 28458 | 332ER | 697 | Delta Air Lines | N1201P | |
| 28495 | 33AER | 643 | City Bird | OO-CTR | |
| 28553 | 346 | 688 | Japan Asia Airways | JA8987 | |
| 28656 | 35DER | 659 | LOT Polish Airlines | SP-LPC | |
| 28745 | 319ER | 677 | Air New Zealand | ZK-NCL | |
| 28837 | 346 | 673 | Japan Air Lines | JA8980 | |
| 28838 | 346 | 680 | Japan Air Lines | JA8986 | |
| 28865 | 31KER | 657 | Airtours | G-DIMB | |
| 28883 | 304ER | | Britannia Airways | | |
| 28884 | 304ER | | Britannia Airways | | |
| 28979 | 304ER | 691 | Britannia Airways | G-OBYE | |
| 29117 | 338ER | 710 | Qantas | VH-OGT | |
| 29118 | 338ER | 713 | Qantas | VH-OGU | |
| 29129 | 38EFER | 693 | Asiana | HL7528 | |
| 29227 | 319ER | 698 | LAN Chile | CC-CZW | |
| 29228 | 319ER | 699 | LAN Chile | CC-CZT | |
| 29230 | 336ER | 702 | British Airways | G-BZHA | |
| 29236 | 322ER | 707 | United Airlines | N664UA | |
| 29237 | 322ER | 711 | United Airlines | N665UA | |
| 29238 | 322ER | 715 | United Airlines | N666UA | |
| 29239 | 322ER | 716 | United Airlines | N667UA | |
| 29429 | 323ER | 700 | American Airlines | N392AN | |
| 29430 | 323ER | 701 | American Airlines | N393AN | |
| 29431 | 323ER | 703 | American Airlines | N394AN | |
| 29432 | 323ER | 709 | American Airlines | N395AN | |
| 29689 | 332ER | 706 | Delta Air Lines | N169DZ | |
| 29690 | 332ER | 717 | Delta Air Lines | N171DZ | |
| 29691 | 332ER | 719 | Delta Air Lines | N172DZ | |
| 29692 | 332ER | 723 | Delta Air Lines | N173DZ | |
| 29693 | 332ER | 725 | Delta Air Lines | N174DZ | |
| 29694 | 332ER | | Delta Air Lines | N175DZ | |
| 29695 | 332ER | | Delta Air Lines | N176DZ | |
| 29696 | 332ER | | Delta Air Lines | N177DZ | |
| 29697 | 332ER | | Delta Air Lines | N178DZ | |
| 29698 | 332ER | | Delta Air Lines | N179DZ | |

New American Airlines 767-323ER N393AW returning from a production test flight at Everett in May 1998 prior to being delivered to the airline in the same month. This was the 700th 767 to be delivered. *Philip Birtles*

# INDEX